PROBLEMS IN CIVILIZATION

CHURCH
AND STATE
IN EUROPE
1864–1914

Edited with
an Introduction by

Ernst C. Helmreich

Bowdoin College

FORUM PRESS

Published simultaneously in Canada.

Printed in the United States of America.

Library of Congress Catalog Card Number: 78-68021

ISBN: 0-88273-405-9

Pius IX (1846-1878)

TABLE OF CONTENTS

INTRODUCTION

CONFLICT OF OPINION

INTRODUCTION

I N THE study of history one is constantly struck by the similarity of issues and problems that are present in all ages. None of these is more thorny than the problem of the relationship between religion and the state. It is far older than Christianity and it is not at all surprising that it has been a continuing issue in the history of the Christian church. Christ did not settle the issue clearly when he admonished the Pharisees to "Render therefore unto Caesar the things which are Caesar's and unto God the things which are God's." The dispute arises over the line of demarcation. During the Middle Ages the theory of the two spheres, the Spiritual and Temporal, was generally accepted but this did not settle the question of supremacy. The state, to be sure, was universally considered a Christian institution obligated to nourish, protect, and further the church. Church law held that the state was obligated to punish heretics, and this obligation was accepted by the state. Among the decretals of Gregory IX in the thirteenth century there is the statement that if a prince refuses to punish heretics, after due warning, he shall be excommunicated and his subjects absolved from their oaths of loyalty. This was an aspect of church-state law which needed readjustment when at the time of the Reformation in the Religious Peace of Augsburg (1555) and in other agreements as well, the state recognized the parity of religious confessions. Catholic princes had regularly attended Church Councils, but when Protestant princes appeared how were they to fit into the picture? This problem was not settled at the Council of Trent (1545-1564). Nor did that Council settle another long-standing question, whether the Pope or the Council was the supreme authority in the church.

While the Catholic Church claimed to be universal, united in doctrine and dogma, it was far from united in church practice, and there was no uniform relationship between Pope, bishops, and rulers. While this flexibility sometimes brought peace to church and state it was also a cause of discontent and jealousy. Whatever concessions one bishop or ruler might have, another might want, while basically in Rome the aim was to achieve centralized uniformity. Within the church, too, in the seventeenth and eighteenth centuries movements arose which attacked the central governing power of the papacy within the church. These movements were opposed by the Jesuits who sought both to strengthen and to control the Papacy.

While the church was torn by dissension and the lack of strong leadership, the state on the whole grew in power. As time went on, new political theories led to the concept of the complete sovereignty of the state. The absolute state came to dominate the church and nowhere was this more complete than in eighteenth century France, where the historic Gallican Liberties of the French church flowered anew. So strong was the position of the state over against the church that the Pope, under coercion from the Catholic kings of Spain, Portugal and France, actually dissolved the Jesuit order in 1773.

The philosophy of the Enlightenment, which ridiculed many old religious concepts and advanced new, rationalistic ideas of religious freedom, favored the increased secularization of society and the power of secular governments. The Enlightened Despot, ruling over both Catholic and Protestant subjects, advocated the religiously neutral state. Frederic II of Prussia had little difficulty in implementing this policy, for it was largely a matter of conceding to Catholics the same privileges which Protestants already enjoyed. In Prussia the supremacy of the state was accepted as a matter of course, but the state, by establishing a collegial system of church government and thereby in a measure sharing its sovereignty, permitted the Protestant churches to be essentially self-governing under the supervision of the state. Frederick was willing to accord this position to Catholics as well but, as always, the supervisory rights of the state were carefully safeguarded. The great Prussian legal codification of 1794 provided that no bishop could make new decrees or receive directives from any foreign ecclesiastical superior without permission of the state, and that all Papal bulls, briefs, or rescripts of alien religious authorities had to have the approval of the state before publication.

These and similar laws were leniently enforced and the Catholic Church was pleased with its status in Prussia.

When Joseph II tried to do much the same thing in the Habsburg lands, he ran into difficulties. Here it was a question of cutting down on the special rights and privileges of the dominant and powerful Catholic Church, granting the Protestant minority a modicum of equality, and establishing the rights of the state. He found it necessary to take far-reaching measures which conflicted with the historic doctrines and practices of the church. So far did Joseph go that the label Josephinism has been given to the principle that the state has complete supremacy over the church. Confiscation of monastic lands and religious toleration were the more spectacular measures, but perhaps even more significant were enactments which required priests to perform mixed marriages without reference to pre-nuptial agreements, forbade bishops to communicate with Rome except through the royal chancelleries, and established complete state control over the appointment of the hierarchy.

The French Revolution had profound effects on the Catholic Church. The Civil Constitution of the Clergy in France established a new relationship between church and state, which after much strife was modified and stabilized in the Concordat of 1801. In spite of this settlement disputes arose between Napoleon and the Pope which led to the incorporation of the Papal States into France. The Pope promptly excommunicated Napoleon, who in turn arrested the Pope and carried him off to France. When the Pope returned to Rome in May 1814 he at once set to work to rebuild the church. The Jesuit Order was restored, the Inquisition in Rome was reestablished and the Index reconstituted, while the Congress of Vienna returned the Papal States to his rule.

The confiscation of church lands, the secularization of ecclesiastical states in Germany, the disappearance of the Holy Roman Empire, the shifting of territorial boundaries which now united Protestant and Catholic regions into one state, the general acceptance of the ideas of constitutionalism with safeguards for religious liberty and other individual rights, and the growing liberal concept of the religiously neutral state pointed to the need for redefining the relationship between church and state. The governments all turned to these problems. The Papacy, anxious to free the church from the state control and supervision of the eighteenth century, sought to achieve a new status by negotiating concordats with various states, in which the rights, privileges, and financial claims of the church were to be guaranteed. A whole series of these agreements was concluded, more in the nineteenth century than in the whole previous history of the church. One of the most significant of these was the Concordat of 1855 with Austria which swept aside most of the remnants of Joseph II's legislation.

Although no concordat was signed with Prussia, the Pope and the Prussian government easily reached an agreement for the establishment of nine dioceses in Prussia, and the state promised more satisfactory financial support. So pleased was the Pope with the settlement that he issued a special bull in which he thanked the Prussian government and compared Frederick William III with Theodosius the Great. Yet in a few years a bitter conflict broke out over the education of children of mixed marriages. The so-called *Kölner Kirchenstreit* (Cologne Church Quarrel) was at its height in the late 1830's, when several bishops were arrested and removed from office. A *modus vivendi* was achieved in 1838 when the state decreed that while the clergy could not exact a formal promise as to the education of the children, the bishop had authority in controversial cases. When Frederick William IV became king in 1840 he sought to establish religious peace by abolishing the *Placet*, that is, the obligation of the church to receive state approval before publishing its decrees in Prussia. He also established separate Catholic and Protestant bureaus in the Ministry of Education and Church Affairs. In effect this meant more autonomy for both Protestant and Catholic churches, and in the Prussian Constitution of 1850 the churches were specifically given the right to regulate their own affairs. The Catholic Church had emerged very well from the Cologne church struggle; in fact its position was far better in the religiously liberal Prussian state than in Catholic Bavaria, where state control of the church still prevailed as in the preceding century.

There were many forces which favored

the church in this restoration period. The rulers sought the support of the churches as a counter to the revolutionary spirit which still hovered over Europe after 1815. There was also a general religious revival in Europe at this time, no doubt in part a reaction against the skepticism of the Enlightenment, as well as a turning to God brought about by the suffering and terror of the revolutionary era. Pietism staged a revival in Germany. The Romantic Movement with its glorification of the Middle Ages tended particularly to strengthen the Catholic Church and its leader. Bishops, who had formerly looked to the state, as a result of the confiscation of their lands and other restrictive legislation had come to realize they could no longer rely on secular aid and turned to the Papacy for support. Ultramontanism (looking over the mountains to the Papacy for leadership), increased within the church itself. Notably in France, writers like du Bonald, Lamennais, and de Maistre were influential in arousing a new interest in Catholicism. In England the Oxford Movement sought an approach to Rome. In Germany there was a group of notable converts to Catholicism, and the Catholic revival was manifest in the tremendous pilgrimages to Trier in 1844 when the "Holy Cloak" was displayed for veneration. To counter the rising influence and manifestation of Catholicism, Thomas Chalmers, a noted Scottish clergyman, was instrumental in organizing the Evangelical Alliance at an international conference in London in 1846. It aimed at bringing believing individuals, not churches, together. In subsequent years periodic large international conferences were held in various cities of the world, and at the meeting in Berlin in 1857 the Prussian king took an active part. The Alliance has maintained itself to the present.

At the same time there were many forces at work which countered the renewed interest in religion. The philosophy of the Enlightenment with its skepticism and its emphasis on rationalism had — in spite of all reaction — undermined ancient religious concepts and practices. Higher criticism of the Bible seemed to threaten the very foundations of religion. To these were added new developments in science. The steadily increasing secularization of society, changing views in regard to the right of the church to control education and marriages, the spread of socialistic ideas, and the rapid growth of political liberalism all added to the growing challenge of old religious concepts. These seemingly anti-church movements appeared to find their climax in the Revolution of 1848. Again the Pope was forced to flee Rome by revolutionary upheaval.

Pius IX returned to Rome in 1850 thoroughly disillusioned with liberalism. As ruler of the Papal States he followed a reactionary policy in these Italian territories. As head of the church he launched a renewed authoritarian policy of centralization. Roman Catholic hierarchies were established in England in 1850 and in the Netherlands in 1854. The Proclamation of the Dogma of the Immaculate Conception in 1854, which was generally accepted without protest by the whole hierarchy and by the faithful, showed how undisputed his leadership within the church had become.

Pius IX issued many encyclicals, letters, and pronouncements condemning existing practices and ideas of the times. Many of these were directly the result of political events in Italy which in 1860 had led to the incorporation of most of the Papal States in the new Italian Kingdom. Finally in 1864 he issued the Encyclical *Quanta Cura*, and appended to it in tabular form his list of eighty common errors of the times. (See Section I.)

Although all the errors had been condemned in previous papal pronouncements and the Pope carefully cited these, the publication of them in a collected list caused consternation throughout the world. (See "The Syllabus: Its Significance?", pages 6—13.) Liberal Catholics who had been hoping to reconcile Catholic teaching and practice with current philosophic and scientific thought, and above all with the new liberal political state, were disconsolate. It was clear that its pronouncements were contrary to the concepts and laws of many of the states. Undismayed, the Pope in 1868 announced the convening of a Church Council. An article published by the authoritative Jesuit-controlled *Civiltà Cattolica* in February, 1869, spoke about confirming in positive form the statements of the Syllabus and proclaiming the infallibility of the Pope. This article created a division in the church between those of the hierarchy who favored and those who opposed declaring the Pope infallible. (See "The Vatican Council," Section I.)

The controversies within the church also created concern in the Protestant world and among the governments of states both Protestant and Catholic. Just what would it mean if the tenets of the Syllabus were declared dogmas of the church? In fact some Catholics already were asserting that the Syllabus had that status. The influential *Dublin Review* as early as 1865 maintained that the Syllabus possessed absolute infallibility, and repeatedly reaffirmed this position. Political leaders worried about the future relations between the state and an infallible Pope whose hierarchy, as a result of the new developments, would be more subservient to papal pronouncements than ever before.

In April 1869 the Prime Minister of Bavaria tried to get the states of Europe to concert their efforts for the protection of their interests at the forthcoming Council, but so firmly had the concept of the religiously neutral state established itself that all the great powers refused to support the Bavarian initiative. The Pope had not issued invitations to the governments to send representatives, which was contrary to precedent. When this was called to the attention of Vatican authorities, they pointed out that the head of one state (the king of Italy) was under excommunication, but if the states wanted to send observers they were welcome to do so after proper notification. No states sent such representatives and the church was left alone to decide its own affairs. When the Council did get under way, however, the proceedings caused alarm among the powers. On January 21, 1870, a *schema de ecclesia* was submitted to the Council which redefined the status of the church. This document asserted that it was an error to maintain that the separation of church and state was beneficial for society and declared anathema those who held that in a civil society the church was subject to secular control. Church control over education was insisted upon and the document concluded with twenty-one canons of anathemas. The *schema* aroused much concern among the governments and led to protests from France and Austria, the two foremost Catholic powers. Bavaria, Portugal, and Prussia formally adhered to these remonstrances, but when the French Foreign Minister, Daru, who had shown the most initiative, was forced out of office, the movement for state

interference with the Council ended. The church fathers were again left to their own deliberations. (See "The Powers and the Vatican Council," pages 21—25.)

Too often attention is so riveted on Papal Infallibility that the very important Dogmatic Constitution of Catholic Faith which was adopted on April 24, 1870, is overlooked. Having dealt with Catholic Faith the Council proceeded to the adoption of the Dogmatic Constitution on the Church of Christ and the Infallibility of the Pope. (See "The Vatican Decrees: Selections," Section I.)

The delegates at the Council were split on the issue of infallibility, but on the whole the clergy of Germany and Austria were opposed, as well as many from France and some from the United States. Archbishop Kendrick of St. Louis was the foremost American opponent. At the cru ̄ ᵢ vote in the secret session with 601 members present 451 voted *Placet*, 88 *non Placet* and 62 conditional *Placet*. In other words 451 were for and 150 against the declaration of infallibility. At the final public session where it was formally adopted, most of the opposing bishops absented themselves and there were only two dissenting votes, that of Bishop Riccio of Cajazzo in Sicily and of Bishop Fitzgerald of Little Rock, Arkansas. In the end all bishops accepted the Doctrine of Infallibility and remained within the church. Bishop Strossmayer of Zagreb was one of the last to do so; he did not proclaim the doctrine in his diocese until 1872.

The Council adjourned on July 18 and the following day the Franco-Prussian War broke out. For the time being world attention was focused on that conflict and the Council which was scheduled to reassemble in October never met again. But repercussions from the Council were not slow in making their appearance. (See "Papal Infallibility: Cause for Alarm?" pages 28—35.) Everywhere controversial articles appeared. W. E. Gladstone, England's great Liberal party leader and famous pamphleteer, jumped into the fray with a ringing discourse on "The Vatican Decrees in Their Bearing on Civil Allegiance." He was answered by Archbishop Manning, a recent convert to Catholicism. In Germany, Professor Johann J. I. von Döllinger, a leading Catholic theologian and Professor of Ecclesiastical History at the University of Munich, led the opposition to the decrees of the Council and helped in organizing the dissident old Catholic church. Other voices of alarm sounded in many countries.

Ever since Austria had started reorganizing its government by the November Patent of 1860, the Austrian leaders, pushed by the German liberals, had tried to negotiate a revision of the Concordat of 1855. The Pope steadily refused to negotiate, but even devout Francis Joseph knew that the concessions he had made to the church in this agreement could not be maintained. The Austrian constitutional laws adopted as part of the *Ausgleich* of 1867, and laws on schools, interconfessional matters, and civil marriage of 1868 were denounced by the Pope as violating the concordat, but he would not sanction a revision of that document. On August 6, 1870, the Austrian government unilaterally cancelled the Concordat of 1855, maintaining that the dogma of infallibility had so changed the character of one of the contracting parties that the concordat could no longer be considered binding. (See note from Count Beust, Section I.) Although there were further controversies between church and state during the next decades in Austria and Hungary, these were carried on with more moderation than in many of the other European states.

Since the seizure of portions of the Papal States in the unification movement of 1859-60 the Papacy had been living in open enmity with the Italian government. The attempt of Cavour and his successors to implement the policy of a "Free Church in a Free State" through legislation had only caused more difficulties. When the Franco-Prussian War brought the withdrawal of French troops from Rome where they had been protecting the Pope, the Italian government, with the overwhelming approval of the Italian people, took over Rome and put an end to the Papal State. Italy attempted in 1871 to placate the Papacy by passing the famous Law of Guarantees, but Pius IX refused to accept the generous settlement and chose to consider himself the Prisoner of the Vatican. (See Jemolo, "The Law of Papal Guarantees," Section II.) The Pope repeatedly denounced the seizure of Rome, and in the next two decades, at least, Vatican diplomacy was obsessed with the attempt to persuade some foreign power to restore Rome to its control. This Roman

Question complicated European affairs and directly or indirectly entered into church-state relations in all states. (See Halperin, "The Continuing Feud," Section II.) The Pope did his best to hamper the new Italian state government and by decree forbade Catholics to vote in parliamentary elections. (See Webster, "Catholics in National Politics," Section II.) Conflict between church and state waxed bitter at times after 1870, and it always bedeviled Italian politics. (See "Acquiescence or Reconciliation," pages 51—57.)

After the Vatican Council, church-state conflict in Austria and Italy was, in reality, only the continuation of difficulties which had started in 1860. In Germany and France the relations between church and state had been relatively peaceful before 1870, but here too conflict now developed.

The Catholics in Germany had generally supported unification on the so-called "large" German basis under the leadership of Austria. Bismarck, however, had brought about unification on a "small" German basis, under the leadership of Protestant Prussia. Prussia had obtained a considerable accession of Catholic population through the war of 1866, and Bismarck was particularly concerned to maintain friendly relations with them. He also wanted to get the predominantly Catholic South German states to join his North German Confederation. This no doubt accounts for his strict hands-off policy towards the Vatican Council. The Franco-Prussian War brought the final establishment of a United Germany, and Bismarck was now determined that nothing was to destroy the unity which had been achieved.

If Protestants in Germany were afraid of what an Infallible Pope would do, Catholics were afraid of what would happen to them as a minority in a United Germany which was largely Protestant. For a time after 1848 there had been a Catholic Political Faction in Prussia, but this had disintegrated. The Catholics now decided to reorganize, and in 1870 founded the Center party. It first made its appearance in Prussia, but soon had affiliates throughout Germany. One of the founders of the party and its great leader in this period was Ludwig Windthorst, formerly Minister of Justice in Hanover.

In the first Imperial Reichstag which met in the fall of 1871 Windthorst led the Center party in an attack on a sentence in the speech from the throne which stated that the new German government would not intervene in the internal affairs of a neighboring state. The Center wanted Germany to take action against Italy in favor of restoring Rome to the Pope. In the same Reichstag the Center advanced a demand that Articles 15, 16, and 18 of the Prussian Constitution, which provided for the autonomy of the Churches, should be incorporated in the new Imperial Constitution. For many reasons Bismarck was opposed to doing this. Religion and educational matters were a concern of the individual states and to have inserted these provisions in the national constitution would have aroused the opposition of some of the state governments. Bismarck wanted to do nothing which would raise the question of states rights in the new Federal Germany. In a speech in the Prussian lower chamber on January 30, 1872, Bismarck permitted himself some words about the Center party. He stated:

From my earliest days I have always considered that one of the worst possible events that could take place was the formation of a confessional party in a political assembly. I can view this party in no other light than as a mobilization against the state.

The Center Party received much support from the representatives of the Polish districts and after 1874 from the representatives of Alsace-Lorraine. Such a combination of Catholics, particularistic Poles and Francophiles, did not appeal to Bismarck. (See Eyck, "The Course of the *Kulturkampf*," Section III.)

It is clear that Bismarck was reluctant to get involved in controversy with the church. Early in the dispute with the Center party, he appointed Cardinal Hohenlohe as German ambassador to the Vatican, believing this to be a conciliatory gesture. Unfortunately both the appointment, without previous consultation with the Pope, and the candidate were displeasing to Pius IX. Cardinal Hohenlohe had been a staunch opponent of Papal Infallibility at the Council, and was anti-Jesuit in sentiment. The Pope refused to accept him as ambassador, and this added to Bismarck's belief that a confessional party threatened the unity of Germany. It was in connection with this incident that Bismarck gave the members of the Reichstag the much-quoted assurance: "Do not be concerned, we shall not go to Canossa, neither bodily nor spiritually." (See Bismarck, pages 65–66.)

A series of laws were shortly enacted cutting down on the privilege of the churches in Prussia. One law called forth another and soon Prussia, and some other German states as well, were involved in a bitter church and state conflict which came to be called the *Kulturkampf*. The name was coined by Dr. Rudolf Virchow (1821–1902), a world-famous pathologist and a man who also found time to engage in politics. In a speech in the Prussian lower chamber on January 17, 1873, during a debate on the law dealing with the education of the clergy, he used the term *Kulturkampf*. The term was repeated in the election manifesto of the Progressive party in March 1873, and it was soon applied to the church-state conflict which was then being waged. To Virchow *Kulturkampf*, however, had a deeper meaning; he used it to express the antagonism between the rising technical civilization and the old cultural concepts which the church was upholding. The struggle for civilization was to achieve the values which the Papacy had condemned in the Syllabus of Errors, and which the victory of the ultramontane party at the Vatican Council seemed to jeopardize. (See Virchow, pages 66–68).

In the next years the bitterness of the struggle increased. Bismarck defined the issue in a notable speech to the Prussian Diet as the age-old conflict between secular and priestly authority (*Königthum* and *Priesterthum*). In 1875 Pius IX declared all the Prussian legislation affecting the church null and void, and threatened anyone who obeyed these laws with excommunication. (See Pius IX, pages 71–72.) The state refused to backtrack; instead it passed more stringent measures.

Such a condition was most unsatisfactory to both the church and the state and both sides sought ways out of the impasse. Finally in 1878 Pius IX died and his successor, Leo XIII, announced his accession to the Papal throne to William I in a conciliatory letter. The German Emperor answered in like terms. The Papacy exercised a moderating influence on the Center party, and Bismarck undertook the repeal and modification of some of the anti-church legislation. (See

Cardinal Jacobini's letters, "Key Documents," and the introductory statement to "Victory, Defeat, or Compromise?" page 74.) By 1887 the conflict was considered ended. Whether Bismarck had gone to Canossa is a disputed point and historians vary in their interpretations. (See "Victory, Defeat, or Compromise?" pages 75—82.)

With the denouement of the controversy in Germany, the center of church-state conflict shifted to France. The Concordat of 1801 had on the whole provided a workable basis for church-state relations in the restoration period. The Falloux law, passed in the early years of the Second Republic (1850), was much more favorable to the church and extended the church's control over the schools. During the Second Empire, Napoleon III continued the policy of making concessions to the clerical parties. It is not surprising that clerical circles were hostile to the Third Republic which was born with defeat in the War of 1870—1871. Liberal republican sentiment became more and more pronouncedly anti-clerical and scored a triumph in the elections of 1876. (See Phillips, "Anti-Clericalism and the Third Republic," Section IV.) Attention was soon focused on educational reform, which was closely entwined with the status of religious orders in France. This led to a series of Laic Laws in the 1880's and ultimately, in the opening years of the twentieth century, to the abrogation of the Concordat of 1801. (See Dansette, "From Laic Laws to Separation," Section IV.)

The conflict between church and state after 1870 led to an extreme radical solution in France. State schools were completely secularized, not only the Jesuits but most of the other religious orders were dissolved, and the complete separation of church and state was decreed. The reasons for this legislation and the significance of the measures are important aspects of the history of the Third Republic. (See "Dechristianization or Religious Revival?" pages 100—109.) On the face of the situation the position of the church in France seemed much less favorable than in either Italy or Germany; whether this was actually the case is debatable. An intelligent answer can only be based on a study of such material as is presented here and in the books suggested for further reading.

CONFLICT OF OPINION

"A complete separation of Church and State would make conciliation and freedom impossible. The peace implicit in Cavour's formula is the peace of the tomb; as well might he have said 'a free soul in a free body.' In fact, conciliation can exist only in the midst of conflict; freedom thrives on struggle. Religion is a social institution, not a mere relationship between Man and God. Religion and the State constitute two exalted spheres of reason, above which — though not outside them — there is only philosophy. They are grounded in a nature or reason that is absolute, determining their relationship and embodying at one and the same time their conflicts, their virtues and their objective reality."

— A. C. Jemolo

"[It is an error to hold that] the Church ought to be separated from the State, and the State from the Church."

— No. 55 of the Syllabus of Errors

"In the relationship between man and religion, the state is firmly committed to a position of neutrality. . . . The breach of neutrality that is today a trickling stream may all too soon become a raging torrent and in the words of Madison, 'it is proper to take alarm at the first experiment on our liberties'."

— Justice Tom C. Clark in *Abington School District v. Schempp* and *Murray v. Curlett*

"Thus this struggle for power [*Kulturkampf*] is subject to the same conditions as every other political struggle, and it is a distortion of the issue, which is intended to influence thoughtless people, when it is represented as if it dealt with the suppression of the church. It has to do with defending the state, it has to do with defining how far the rule of the priesthood and how far the rule of the king shall go, and this demarcation must be such that the state for its part can exist with it. For in the realm of this world the state has rule and precedence."

— Bismarck

"Absolute obedience, it is boldly declared, is due to the Pope, at the peril of Salvation, not alone in faith, in morals, but in all things which concern the discipline and government of the Church. Thus are swept into the Papal net whole multitudes of facts, whole systems of government. . . ."

— William Ewart Gladstone

". . . the Civil allegiance of Catholics is as undivided as that of all Christians, and of all men who recognize a divine or moral law."

— Archbishop Manning

". . . subservience to the ideal of a highly centralized national state may produce intolerance, violation of civil liberties, and suppression of the rights of autonomous groups within the state."

— Evelyn M. Acomb

I. THE ROMAN CATHOLIC CHURCH: MID-NINETEENTH CENTURY DEVELOPMENTS

The Syllabus of Errors

PIUS IX

It is often the practice to quote only a few of the eighty errors listed by the Pope. Here the whole list is presented, for it was exactly its wide coverage which aroused so much attention and consternation in the world at that time. It should be borne in mind that the document as a whole is negative in form and that belief in any of the statements as here formulated is condemned. The translation used by Mr. Gladstone and here presented was actually made by Bishop Manning. Another translation may be conveniently found in Raymond Corrigan, *The Church and the Nineteenth Century* (Milwaukee: Bruce, 1938), pp. 289–295.

I. PANTHEISM, NATURALISM, AND ABSOLUTE RATIONALISM

1. There exists no supreme, most wise, and most provident divine being distinct from the universe, and God is none other than nature, and is therefore subject to change. In effect, God is produced in man and in the world, and all things are God, and have the very substance of God. God is therefore one and the same thing with the world, and thence spirit is the same thing with matter, necessity with liberty, true with false, good with evil, justice with injustice.

2. All action of God upon man and the world is to be denied.

3. Human reason, without any regard to God, is the sole arbiter of truth and falsehood, of good and evil; it is its own law to itself, and suffices by its natural force to secure the welfare of men and of nations.

4. All the truths of religion are derived from the native strength of human reason; where reason is the master rule by which man can and ought to arrive at the knowledge of all truths of every kind.

5. Divine revelation is imperfect, and, therefore, subject to a continual and indefinite progress, which corresponds with the progress of human reason.

6. Christian faith contradicts human reason, and divine revelation not only does not benefit, but even injures the perfection of man.

7. The prophecies and miracles set forth and narrated in the Sacred Scriptures are the fictions of poets; and the mysteries of the Christian faith are the result of philosophical investigations. In the books of both Testaments there are contained mythi-

From W. E. Gladstone and Philip Schaff, *The Vatican Decrees in their Bearing on Civil Allegiance. A Political Expostulation. To which are added: A History of the Vatican Council together with the Latin and English Text of the Papal Syllabus and the Vatican Decrees* (New York: Harper and Brothers, 1875.) The footnotes which the Pope appended to each statement of error are here omitted. The citations in Section IV indicate the character of these notes. Similarly the footnotes which appear in the original publications are omitted from all the other readings here presented.

cal inventions, and Jesus Christ is himself a mythical fiction.

II. MODERN RATIONALISM

8. As human reason is placed on a level with religion, so theological matters must be treated in the same manner as philosophical ones.

9. All the dogmas of the Christian religion are, without exception, the object of scientific knowledge or philosophy, and human reason, instructed solely by history, is able, by its own natural strength and principles, to arrive at the true knowledge of even the most abstruse dogmas: provided such dogmas be proposed as subject-matter for human reason.

10. As the philosopher is one thing, and philosophy is another, so it is the right and duty of the philosopher to submit to the authority which he shall have recognized as true; but philosophy neither can nor ought to submit to any authority.

11. The Church not only ought never to animadvert upon philosophy, but ought to tolerate the errors of philosophy, leaving to philosophy the care of their correction.

12. The decrees of the Apostolic See and of the Roman Congregations fetter the free progress of science.

13. The method and principles by which the old scholastic doctors cultivated theology are no longer suitable to the demands of the age and the progress of science.

14. Philosophy must be treated of without any account being taken of supernatural revelation.

III. INDIFFERENTISM, LATITUDINARIANISM

15. Every man is free to embrace and profess the religion he shall believe true, guided by the light of reason.

16. Men may in any religion find the way of eternal salvation, and obtain eternal salvation.

17. We may entertain at least a well-founded hope for the eternal salvation of all those who are in no manner in the true Church of Christ.

18. Protestantism is nothing more than another form of the same true Christian religion, in which it is possible to be equally pleasing to God as in the Catholic Church.

IV. SOCIALISM, COMMUNISM, SECRET SOCIETIES, BIBLICAL SOCIETIES, CLERICO-LIBERAL SOCIETIES

Pests of this description are frequently rebuked in the severest terms in the Encyc. *Qui pluribus*, Nov. 9, 1846; Alloc. *Quibus quantisque*, April 20, 1849; Encyc. *Noscitis et Nobiscum*, Dec. 8, 1849; Alloc. *Singulari quâdam*, Dec. 9, 1854; Encyc. *Quanto conficiamur moerore*, Aug. 10, 1863.

V. ERRORS CONCERNING THE CHURCH AND HER RIGHTS

19. The Church is not a true, and perfect, and entirely free society, nor does she enjoy peculiar and perpetual rights conferred upon her by her Divine Founder, but it appertains to the civil power to define what are the rights and limits with which the Church may exercise authority.

20. The ecclesiastical power must not exercise its authority without the permission and assent of the civil government.

21. The Church has not the power of defining dogmatically that the religion of the Catholic Church is the only true religion.

22. The obligation which binds Catholic teachers and authors applies only to those things which are proposed for universal belief as dogmas of the faith, by the infallible judgment of the Church.

23. The Roman Pontiffs and oecumenical Councils have exceeded the limits of their power, have usurped the rights of princes, and have even committed errors in defining matters of faith and morals.

24. The Church has not the power of availing herself of force, or any direct or indirect temporal power.

25. In addition to the authority inherent in the Episcopate, a further and temporal

power is granted to it by the civil authority, either expressly or tacitly, which power is on that account also revocable by the civil authority whenever it pleases.

26. The Church has not the innate and legitimate right of acquisition and possession.

27. The ministers of the Church, and the Roman Pontiff, ought to be absolutely excluded from all charge and dominion over temporal affairs.

28. Bishops have not the right of promulgating even their apostolical letters, without the permission of the government.

29. Dispensations granted by the Roman Pontiff must be considered null, unless they have been asked for by the civil government.

30. The immunity of the Church and of ecclesiastical persons derives its origin from civil law.

31. Ecclesiastical courts for temporal causes, of the clergy, whether civil or criminal, ought by all means to be abolished, either without the concurrence and against the protest of the Holy See.

32. The personal immunity exonerating the clergy from military service may be abolished, without violation either of natural right or of equity. Its abolition is called for by civil progress, especially in a community constituted upon principles of liberal government.

33. It does not appertain exclusively to ecclesiastical jurisdiction, by any right, proper and inherent, to direct the teaching of theological subjects.

34. The teaching of those who compare the sovereign Pontiff to a free sovereign acting in the universal Church is a doctrine which prevailed in the middle ages.

35. There would be no obstacle to the sentence of a general council, or the act of all the universal peoples, transferring the pontifical sovereignty from the Bishop and City of Rome to some other bishopric and some other city.

36. The definition of a national council does not admit of any subsequent discussion, and the civil power can regard as settled an affair decided by such national council.

37. National churches can be established, after being withdrawn and plainly separated from the authority of the Roman Pontiff.

38. Roman Pontiffs have, by their too arbitrary conduct, contributed to the division of the Church into eastern and western.

VI. ERRORS ABOUT CIVIL SOCIETY, CONSIDERED BOTH IN ITSELF AND IN ITS RELATION TO THE CHURCH

39. The commonwealth is the origin and source of all rights, and possesses rights which are not circumscribed by any limits.

40. The teaching of the Catholic Church is opposed to the well-being and interests of society.

41. The civil power, even when exercised by an unbelieving sovereign, possesses an indirect and negative power over religious affairs. It therefore possesses not only the right called that of *exequatur,* but that of the (so-called) *appellatio ab abusu.*

42. In the case of conflicting laws between the two powers, the civil law ought to prevail.

43. The civil power has a right to break, and to declare and render null, the conventions (commonly called *Concordats*) concluded with the Apostolic See, relative to the use of rights appertaining to the ecclesiastical immunity, without the consent of the Holy See, and even contrary to its protest.

44. The civil authority may interfere in matters relating to religion, morality, and spiritual government. Hence it has control over the instructions for the guidance of consciences issued, conformably with their mission, by the pastors of the Church. Further, it possesses power to decree, in the matter of administering the divine sacraments, as to the dispositions necessary for their reception.

45. The entire direction of public schools, in which the youth of Christian states are educated, except (to a certain extent) in the case of episcopal seminaries, may and must appertain to the civil power, and belong to it so far that no other authority whatsoever shall be recognized as having any right to interfere in the discipline of the schools, the arrangement of the studies, the taking of degrees, or the choice and approval of the teachers.

46. Much more, even in clerical seminaries, the method of study to be adopted is subject to the civil authority.

47. The best theory of civil society requires that popular schools open to the children of all classes, and, generally, all public institutes intended for instruction in letters and philosophy, and for conducting the education of the young, should be freed from all ecclesiastical authority, government, and interference, and should be fully subject to the civil and political power, in conformity with the will of rulers and the prevalent opinions of the age.

48. This system of instructing youth, which consists in separating it from the Catholic faith and from the power of the Church, and in teaching exclusively, or at least primarily, the knowledge of natural things and the earthly ends of social life alone, may be approved by Catholics.

49. The civil power has the right to prevent ministers of religion, and the faithful, from communicating freely and mutually with each other, and with the Roman Pontiff.

50. The secular authority possesses, as inherent in itself, the right of presenting bishops, and may require of them that they take possession of their dioceses before having received canonical institution and the apostolic letters from the Holy See.

51. And, further, the secular government has the right of deposing bishops from their pastoral functions, and it is not bound to obey the Roman Pontiff in those things which relate to episcopal sees and the institution of bishops.

52. The government has of itself the right to alter the age prescribed by the Church for the religious profession, both of men and women; and it may enjoin upon all religious establishments to admit no person to take solemn vows without its permission.

53. The laws for the protection of religious establishments, and securing their rights and duties, ought to be abolished: nay, more, the civil government may lend its assistance to all who desire to quit the religious life they have undertaken, and break their vows. The government may also suppress religious orders, collegiate churches, and simple benefices, even those belonging to private patronage, and submit their goods and revenues to the administration and disposal of the civil power.

54. Kings and princes are not only exempt from the jurisdiction of the Church, but are superior to the Church, in litigated questions of jurisdiction.

55. The Church ought to be separated from the State, and the State from the Church.

VII. ERRORS CONCERNING NATURAL AND CHRISTIAN ETHICS

56. Moral laws do not stand in need of the divine sanction, and there is no necessity that human laws should be conformable to the law of nature, and receive their sanction from God.

57. Knowledge of philosophical things and morals, and also civil laws, may and must depart from divine and ecclesiastical authority.

58. No other forces are to be recognized than those which reside in matter; and all moral teaching and moral excellence ought to be made to consist in the accumulation and increase of riches by every possible means, and in the enjoyment of pleasure.

59. Right consists in the material fact, and all human duties are but vain words, and all human acts have the force of right.

60. Authority is nothing else but the result of numerical superiority and material force.

61. An unjust act, being successful, inflicts no injury upon the sanctity of right.

62. The principle of *non-intervention*, as it is called, ought to be proclaimed and ahered to.

63. It is allowable to refuse obedience to legitimate princes: nay, more, to rise in insurrection against them.

64. The violation of a solemn oath, even every wicked and flagitious action repugnant to the eternal law, is not only not blamable, but quite lawful, and worthy of the highest praise, when done for the love of country.

VIII. THE ERRORS CONCERNING CHRISTIAN MARRIAGE

65. It can not be by any means tolerated, to maintain that Christ has raised marriage to the dignity of a sacrament.

66. The sacrament of marriage is only an adjunct of the contract, and separable from it, and the sacrament itself consists in the nuptial benediction alone.

67. By the law of nature, the marriage tie is not indissoluble, and in many cases divorce, properly so called, may be pronounced by the civil authority.

68. The Church has not the power of laying down what are diriment impediments to marriage. The civil authority does possess such a power, and can do away with existing impediments to marriage.

69. The Church only commenced in later ages to bring in diriment impediments, and then availing herself of a right not her own, but borrowed from the civil power.

70. The canons of the Council of Trent, which pronounce censure and anathema against those who deny to the Church the right of laying down what are diriment impediments, either are not dogmatic, or must be understood as referring only to such borrowed power.

71. The form of solemnizing marriage prescribed by the said Council, under penalty of nullity, does not bind in cases where the civil law has appointed another form, and where it decrees that this new form shall effectuate a valid marriage.

72. Boniface VIII is the first who declared that the vow of chastity pronounced at ordination annuls nuptials.

73. A merely civil contract may, among Christians, constitute a true marriage; and it is false, either that the marriage contract between Christians is always a sacrament, or that the contract is null if the sacrament be excluded.

74. Matrimonial causes and espousals belong by their very nature to civil jurisdiction.

IX. ERRORS REGARDING THE CIVIL POWER OF THE SOVEREIGN PONTIFF

75. The children of the Christian and Catholic Church are not agreed upon the compatibility of the temporal with the spiritual power.

76. The abolition of the temporal power, of which the Apostolic See is possessed, would contribute in the greatest degree to the liberty and prosperity of the Church.

X. ERRORS HAVING REFERENCE TO MODERN LIBERALISM

77. In the present day, it is no longer expedient that the Catholic religion shall be held as the only religion of the State, to the exclusion of all other modes of worship.

78. Whence it has been wisely provided by law, in some countries called Catholic, that persons coming to reside therein shall enjoy the public exercise of their own worship.

79. Moreover, it is false that the civil liberty of every mode of worship, and the full power given to all of overtly and publicly manifesting their opinions and their ideas, of all kinds whatsoever, conduce more easily to corrupt the morals and minds of the people, and to the propagation of the pest of indifferentism.

80. The Roman Pontiff can and ought to reconcile himself to, and agree with, progress, liberalism, and civilization as lately introduced.

The Syllabus: Its Significance

The Syllabus aroused much furor and discussion. What was its relation to the doctrine and dogma of the church? What was its significance in relation to the liberal scientific thought of the day, and to the modern concept of the sovereignty of the state? Here four statements on the Syllabus are presented. The first is an authoritative Catholic statement on its binding power and importance; the second is by an English historian who has written extensively on Papal and Italian history and whose biography of Pius IX bears the imprimatur of Cardinal Spellman; the third is by a liberal English historian who in 1912 published what is still one of the best and most comprehensive studies of the Risorgimento; the fourth is by a foremost American church historian, for many years Professor of Missions and Oriental History at Yale, who published numerous volumes on the history of Christianity. Comments on the Syllabus will also appear in subsequent selections on the Vatican Council and on events in the various countries of Europe.

The Syllabus: Its Power and Importance

THE CATHOLIC ENCYCLOPEDIA

THE binding power of the Syllabus of Pius IX is differently explained by Catholic theologians. All are of the opinion that many of the propositions are condemned if not in the Syllabus, then certainly in other final decisions of the infallible teaching authority of the Church, for instance in the Encyclical "Quanta Cura." There is no agreement, however, on the question whether each thesis condemned in the Syllabus is infallibly false, merely because it is condemned in the Syllabus. Many theologians are of the opinion that to the Syllabus as such an infallible teaching authority is to be ascribed, whether due to an ex-cathedra decision by the pope or to the subsequent acceptance by the Church. Others question this. So long as Rome has not decided the question, everyone is free to follow the opinion he chooses. Even should the condemnation of many propositions not possess that unchangeableness

peculiar to infallible decisions, nevertheless the binding force of the condemnation in regard to all the propositions is beyond doubt. For the Syllabus, as appears from the official communication of Cardinal Antonelli, is a decision given by the pope speaking as universal teacher and judge to Catholics the world over. All Catholics, therefore, are bound to accept the Syllabus. Exteriorly they may neither in word nor in writing oppose its contents; they must also assent to it interiorly. . . .

The importance of the Syllabus lies in its opposition to the high tide of that intellectual movement of the nineteenth century which strove to sweep away the foundations of all human and Divine order. The Syllabus is not only the defense of the inalienable rights of God, of the Church, and of truth against the abuse of the words *freedom* and *culture* on the part of unbridled Liberalism, but it is also a pro-

From the article on "The Syllabus of Pius IX" by A. Haag in *The Catholic Encyclopedia*, Vol. XIV, pp. 368–9. Reprinted by permission of The Catholic University of America Press.

test, earnest and energetic, against the attempt to eliminate the influence of the Catholic Church on the life of nations and of individuals, on the family and the school. In its nature, it is true, the Syllabus is negative and condemnatory; but it received its complement in the decisions of the Vatican Council and in the Encyclicals of Leo XIII. It is precisely its fearless character that perhaps accounts for its influence on the life of the Church towards the end of the nineteenth century; for it threw a sharp, clear light upon reef and rock in the intellectual currents of the time.

A Reply to Italy and Modern Liberalism

E. E. Y. HALES

THE Syllabus of Errors and the Encyclical *Quanta Cura* which accompanied it are formidable documents, sweeping in their denunciations, and harsh in tone; they were profoundly upsetting to many within the Church and to others outside who were friendly disposed to her. They gave most satisfaction to the more authoritarian party within and to the more ardently hostile without. To the former they seemed to give official justification; to the latter they seemed so completely unreasonable and absurd as to spell the doom of the Papacy.

They were therefore documents of some consequence, in one sense of even greater consequence than the two dogmas defined in Pio Nono's pontificate, the Immaculate Conception and Papal Infallibility, because those definitions only made dogmatic what the Church as a whole believed, whereas the Encyclical and the Syllabus plunged — though not with dogmatic force — into the most controversial problems of thought and politics. So wide were their implications and repercussions that it is wise, before considering them, to recollect within what limits and having what immediate purposes Rome issued them. The immediate purpose of the Encyclical was to announce a Jubilee, during the following year, 1865, when a plenary indulgence might be gained. It is not long, and, while it runs over much of the same ground as the Syllabus, and condemns most of the same ideas and teaching, it does so in terms which, though indignant, are measured and conventional in form; had it been issued by itself it would probably have attracted little more attention than that small measure which it is usual for Encyclicals to meet, and would have taken its place along with others issued by Pio Nono or with Gregory XVI's *Mirari vos*, which had condemned, in 1832, the principles of Lamennais' *Avenir*.

But the Syllabus was another matter. It was sent out together with the Encyclical. . . .

Of all the condemned propositions, it was number 80 which caused the most stir. It reads as follows: "The Roman Pontiff can and should reconcile and harmonise himself with progress, with liberalism, and with recent civilisation." Like all other propositions it is stigmatised as an error, and the Allocution from which the condemnation is drawn is that *Jamdudum Cernimus* of March 18th, 1861, with which, as we have seen, the Pope con-

From E. E. Y. Hales, *Pio Nono. A Study in European Politics and Religion in the Nineteenth Century* (New York: P. J. Kenedy & Sons, 1954), pp. 255, 258–259, 273–275; 325–326. Reprinted by permission of the publisher.

cluded all idea that he would treat with Cavour about the Temporal Power, or about the setting up of a new relationship between Church and State. Coming at the end of the series, and seeming, in some sort, to sum up the whole, it appeared, in England, or Belgium, or France, to be an anathema hurled at the most cherished ideals of the nineteenth century. Actually, as reference to the Encyclical from which it is drawn shows, it was the Piedmontese government's idea of what constituted progress and civilisation with which the Pope was declining to come to terms. Similarly, the Clerical-Liberal societies which are condemned under proposition 18 are found to be those groups of dissident clergy, in Piedmont, who were opposed to the attitude of Rome about the Siccardi laws, or the closure of the monasteries, or the Temporal Power. . . .

These are examples of errors denounced in the Syllabus which had specific reference to Italy. But in a wider sense most of the Syllabus was prompted by the Italian situation. Pio Nono was witnessing, in Italy, the practical results, as he saw it, of atheist, rationalist, pantheist, or protestant propaganda, of secret societies, of indifferentism, of a wrong view of the relations between the Church and the State. In a sense it was almost all a cri-de-coeur against the Turin government and its religious and political works; but it was a cri-de-coeur, too, against Mazzini. Mazzini at Rome was not forgotten; and Mazzini, in the wake of Garibaldi, was still, behind the Piedmontese, a likely enough heir to the leadership of that United Italy which he had been the first to preach. Nobody had taught about progress, or liberalism, or recent civilisation, with greater eloquence or sincerity, or interpreted those concepts in a less Catholic sense than the sometime Triumvir and prophet of the new religion of God and the People.

Piedmont, and Mazzini. When to these are added the fanatical extravagances of Garibaldi, who was now talking of the Papacy as the "Cancer of Italy", and all the other iconoclastic elements in the risorgimento, together with the not negligible progress of protestantism, especially in Piedmont and Tuscany, and the increased prestige and influence of Italian Freemasonry, it will be recognised how naturally the publication of the Syllabus followed upon the Pope's view of the state of affairs amongst Italians.

But it is equally natural that Europeans as a whole did not interpret the Syllabus as though they were Italians. Every Italian knew that "Progress, Liberalism, and Recent Civilisation" meant the closure of the convents and monasteries, and the imposition of secular education. It meant railways, too, of course, and street lighting by gas, and all those improvements which so interested men like Pasolini, Minghetti, or Cavour; but Italians were not likely to put such matters in the forefront of their thinking; in their context in controversy the terms stood for secularism and anti-clericalism. In England, however, Progress and Recent Civilisation meant primarily the Great Exhibition of 1851, while Liberalism meant conservatives like Peel or Mr. Gladstone who had very few counterparts in Italy. The French interpretation of the phrases was more analogous to the Italian, meaning, to most men, the "Principles of 1789" or just "the Revolution." But in America the words stood, of course, for all that was held most sacred. The question inevitably poses itself whether words capable of such various interpretation, and drawn from an encyclical specifically reprimanding the overrunning of Umbria and the Marches, should have been used as the conclusion to a Syllabus sent to Bishops at Birmingham and New York.

The hierarchies of most western countries found themselves embarrassed in their relations with their governments and with public opinion as a consequence of the Syllabus. That might well be a small matter; but to meet a situation in which "the majority of Catholics were stupefied" was a big one, and particularly big in December, 1864, because some of the greatest leaders of Catholic thought in Europe, and notably Montalembert, had recently been engaged in urging politico-religious concepts of a kind that were specifically reprobated in the Syllabus. With much of the Syllabus, of course, there was no quarrel on the part of Catholics or of other Christians. Thus it condemned propositions such as the denial of the Divinity of Christ, or the validity of Atheism, which any Christian teacher would condemn. But it also condemned certain propositions which were not only generally held outside the Catholic Church but were also widely held within it, and the most controversial of these related to the concept of Toleration. Thus the Syllabus condemned the propositions that: "in our age it is no longer expedient that the Catholic Religion should be regarded as the sole religion of the State to the exclusion of all others" (No. 77); that "The Church has not the power to employ force nor any temporal power direct or indirect" (No. 24); and that everybody should be free to give public utterance, in every possible shape, by every possible channel, to all his notions whatsoever, an attitude which was held to lead to "corruption of manners and minds" and to the "pest of indifferentism" (No. 79). These condemnations were generally taken to mean that religious toleration and freedom of speech were condemned.

The answer of the Church to those who criticised the Pope's teaching on toleration and the explanation given to the bewildered faithful were supplied by Dupanloup in his pamphlet *The September Convention and the Encyclical of December 8*. The indefatigable Bishop of Orleans received the thanks of no less than 630 Bishops for this pamphlet, as well as the approval of the Pope. Dupanloup's line of argument at once brought to light the background against which any series of pontifical statements of principle must be seen, namely that the Pope was talking in terms of absolute and eternal principle, or of "the perfect society", not of what at a given time in any given country might be either expedient or even just. Her enemies were laying down principles which they conceived and claimed were of universal and eternal validity; the Church was denying that they had such validity. Thus in condemning the claims of the Rationalists, she was denying the absolute supremacy of Reason, without Faith, not the validity of Reason as such, or as the ally of Faith; and in condemning the claim to absolute freedom of belief, worship, speech, and press, she was saying that she could not contemplate, as the ultimate ideal, a society which held false beliefs, or tolerated propaganda against the sacraments or other essentials of Catholic practice, or which taught such errors in speech or print. The "true society" would not do these things, and it was therefore erroneous to teach their acceptance as an ultimate ideal. Further, she was saying that in some Catholic countries it would be wrong, even at that day, to disestablish Catholicism and to permit other Churches (this condemnation comes from an Encyclical concerned with Spain); while in others it might be wrong to try to hold on to the privileges of establishment. Throughout Dupanloup's pamphlet runs the distinction between the *thèse* (the ideal of the true society) and the *antithèse* (what is possible or just in the existing state of society). Her opponents were talking in terms of absolutes; so the Church had to make clear what were the true absolutes, or at least must deny those that were false. The great mistake was to suppose that when she condemned a proposition on the absolute plane there might not, yet, be much relative good in it, and that some measure of its practice might not often be healthy and beneficial. And when the absolute claims of a proposition were denied it by no means followed that the contrary proposition was always valid — thus it was erroneous to say that the Catholic Church should everywhere be disestablished, but it was not true to say that she should always be an Established Church.

This relativism was valid argument, even

if to those who looked upon the Church only as one amongst competing "interests" it seemed like opportunism. Nor was the criticism that Dupanloup was "watering down the Syllabus" a fair one; he was arguing in strict accord with the implied thought of the Church; and if the lay press considered him specious he was entitled to reply that the Syllabus had not been addressed to them but presupposed an audience familiar with the terms of theological argument.

It has often been found necessary to curtail liberty in time of crisis, and the Pope had reason to consider this was a time of crisis for the Church. But it is equally important, in such circumstances, not to add fuel to the fire of hostility, and this he unfortunately did by the form in which he allowed the Syllabus to be issued. It is not sufficient to say that the document was technical, and intended only for the Bishops (although this explains much) because the rumor of its issue had reached too far, in advance. And for the same reason it is not sufficient to say that he was thinking mainly of Italy, or that he may have personally concerned himself little with the form it took. It shocked the world, unnecessarily, and Pio Nono, who was always reluctant to shock those whose intentions he recognised as good, was himself distressed by this outcome though he retracted nothing. According to de Falloux he admitted that the Syllabus was "raw meat, needing to be cooked and seasoned." But was it wise to provide raw meat for an enemy, especially an enemy with such an appetite? Why did he leave it to be cooked and seasoned at Orleans, when there were chefs at Rome as skillful?

The Syllabus was widely regarded as a gesture of defiance hurled by an outraged Pope against the nineteenth century. The summoning of the Vatican Council was suspected of being intended to reinforce the Syllabus, and when it defined the dogma of Papal Infallibility it was taken as having done so. Such was the broad interpretation placed upon these events, notably by Gladstone and by Bismarck.

What was the reality?

The Syllabus, though issued to the whole Episcopate and intended for the Church's general guidance, had been prompted, as we have seen, by events in Italy. Does this, then, mean that we are to escape from saying that the Pope was condemning his age as a whole by saying that he was only condemning the risorgimento? Clearly not; the importance of the risorgimento, religiously speaking, was that it was the mirror through which the Pope saw and judged the nostrums of his age; — if there was talk of "a free Church in a free State" his mind naturally leapt to Cavour or to Ricasoli rather than to Montalembert. But on the whole the risorgimento was a faithful mirror of the age because it reflected most of the varied thought and activity and the overweening self-confidence of the European nineteenth century.

What Pio Nono saw reflected in the risorgimento, and what he condemned in the Syllabus, was none other than a mighty wave that threatened, perhaps more dangerously than any previous wave, to submerge the barque of Peter altogether; he saw reflected no less than the rationalism, pantheism, and naturalism of the eighteenth century, the "principles of '89," the new notions of popular sovereignty and human self-sufficiency which sprang from Rousseau and Voltaire. But he would not have seen the danger so clearly if he had not had to suffer from it, personally, at Rome.

Seen in its wider aspect, then, the Syllabus was a reply — an interim reply — to the eighteenth-century "enlightenment" incarnate in the French revolution and the risorgimento; what people like Prince Napoleon boasted of as "Modern Civilisation." But what greatly excited and perturbed friend as well as foe, between 1864 and 1870, was how much of the Syllabus was to be given precise, positive and dogmatic significance. The difficulty was that it embodied such a wide range of condemnations, denouncing, in surprising juxtaposition, obvious heresies such as atheism and more ambiguous notions such as the assertion that the Church could manage very well without the Temporal Power. Once it was known, in 1867, that a General Council of the Church was, indeed, to meet at the end of 1869, it became a source of dread for some — though an aspiration for others — that all the condemnations of the Syllabus, including the more ambiguous ones of a political nature, would be given positive dogmatic precision. There seemed, for example, a likelihood that the Church was not to rest content with teaching, negatively, as in the Syllabus, that it was an error to say that a free press should be introduced universally, but was about to teach, positively, that to allow a free press was always wrong.

There were those who hoped that a wholesale dogmatising of the Syllabus was precisely what the Vatican Council would do, that it would even make belief in the necessity of the Temporal Power dogmatic. It did, however, nothing of the kind. In the Constitution *Dei Filius* it gave dogmatic precision to matters of traditionally accepted faith, concerning the nature of God, and of Revelation, which had been denied, for example, by the Deists and the Pantheists; in this strictly theological field it did "dogmatise" some of the denunciations of the Syllabus. And it defined the dogma of Papal Infallibility, which was another traditionally accepted belief of the Church. But the relations of Church and State, though down for discussion, were never in fact discussed; nor were the problems surrounding political liberty, religious liberty, and freedom of expression; nor were the "principles of '89," nor was the Temporal Power.

In the pontificate of Pio Nono the Church, vis-à-vis Society, was on the defensive. In their various ways Rationalists, Nationalists, Liberals and the rest were laying claims to men's allegiance that were new and the Pope — most notably in the Syllabus of Errors — was condemning these claims in the sense that he was rejecting the notion that their doctrines offered an alternative means of salvation to that offered by the Church. Within the framework of the Church's teaching the new ideas might have validity; on the political plane they might be useful; but in antithesis to the Church's teaching, and offered as a philosophical alternative, they were anathema. In so far as men like Mazzini, or Proudhon, or Bakunin (operating on a wide front in Italy), or Marx, or Treitschke, or, on the political plane, Napoleon, Cavour, or Bismarck represented "modern society" — and in the accepted sense they did — the Pope was prepared to say that he would not be reconciled with modern society; nor would he be reconciled with Progress or Liberalism as those ideas were manifesting themselves around him, whether in the risorgimento, or in Germany, or in the anti-clericalism of the republicans in France. So, in an important sense, he did throw down the gage to modern civilisation; but he threw it down in the Syllabus of Errors, not at the Vatican Council which was irrelevant to the issue; and he threw it down against movements and tendencies which may have had good in them, but which were showing themselves in so hostile and arrogant a light during the last years of his life, after 1870, that he felt no occasion, in his closing years, to withdraw, but rather to emphasize afresh his strictures.

A Challenge to Progress

BOLTON KING

United by a forced conformity within, the church threw down the gauntlet to progress. The Encyclical *Quanta cura* and the Syllabus, or summary of false opinions, that accompanied it (December 8, 1864) mark the divorce that the Ultramontanes had made between the Papacy and civilized government. It is an error, says the Syllabus, that "the Pope can or ought to be reconciled to or compromise with progress or liberalism or modern civilization." The Syllabus is in part an attack on modern thought and criticism; in part a condemnation of the Catholic Reformers, which left no place within the church for those who disbelieved in the Temporal Power, or held to the Free Church, or claimed independent thought in matters of church discipline. But it was perhaps more than all these a root-and-branch onslaught on the principles of free government. It condemned religious toleration in Catholic countries, secular schools, civil marriage and divorce. Legal security for liberty of conscience and worship, said the Encyclical, is "liberty of perdition." The Syllabus implicitly claimed for the Church the right to use temporal punishments, and demanded that the clergy should share in controlling the schools and choosing the teachers, that the ecclesiastical courts should be restored, that the state should surrender its right to nominate bishops. In its full medievalism it asserted the independence of the ecclesiastical power, the divine origin of the church's laws, and their supremacy over any lay legislation.

Whatever may be the precise doctrinal value of the Encyclical and Syllabus, they were rightly taken by the common sense of Europe as a condemnation of liberal government, and a threat that the church would use its strength to combat it. It was the language of men who had cut themselves adrift from reason, and put their trust in the powers of fear and superstition; and those loyal Catholics, who had touch with the world about them, could only put out half-ashamed apologies for its blind and senseless fury. Civilized government was bound to protest against doctrines that struck at its roots. The French government did not conceal its anger, and so strong was the feeling in the country, that Dupanloup had to explain away the most reactionary theses of the Syllabus. In Italy it fanned to flame the smouldering feeling, which wrecked every attempt of the government to conciliate Rome by concession. The resentment, that all Italian patriots felt, had often passed into a virulent hostility, that inspired Garibaldi's passionate invectives, and made a democratic paper declare that the "ultimate end of the Italian revolution was the destruction of the church."

From Bolton King, *A History of Italian Unity Being a Political History of Italy from 1814 to 1871* (London: James Nisbet & Co., 2 vols., 1912), vol. II, pp. 272–273. Reprinted by permission of the publisher.

A Rallying Point for the Faithful

KENNETH SCOTT LATOURETTE

THE Syllabus aroused a storm of criticism in the secular and Protestant press. It produced something like consternation among many who wished to remain within the Roman Catholic Church but were seeking ways of reconciling the Christian faith with the currents of thought and the political theories and movements which were a part of the revolution. In denouncing the ideal of a "free church in a free state" Pius IX was slapping down those who wished by that device to make secure a place for the Roman Catholic Church in the revolutionary world. In condemning the demand that as head of the Roman Catholic Church the Pope take the lead in adjusting the Christian faith to the revolution, Pius seemed to many to be piloting the bark of Peter towards shipwreck.

Yet in contrast with the criticism and the sorrowful protests with which it was greeted, the Syllabus had its staunch defenders. They welcomed it as a courageous attempt to stem the tide towards unbelief.

The net effect of the Syllabus of Errors was to widen and deepen the gulf between the Roman Catholic Church and the revolution and to rally the faithful to the defense and support of the Christian faith as interpreted by that church. In the main Pius IX was keeping the bark of Peter in the course which it had held across the centuries. He was applying to current conditions principles and claims which earlier Popes had been asserting as of the essence of the Christian faith. To him and to the Roman Catholic Church there gathered a following, numbering millions, increasingly knit together under the direction of himself and his successors, aware of the enmity of the world about them, even glorying in it and the attendant conflicts and martyrdoms, and, far from being solely on the defensive, seeking to win that world to the faith.

The next Pope, as we shall see, sought to find points of contact with that world and to influence it in ways consistent with the faith of the Roman Catholic Church, but the positions taken so frankly by Pius IX were never explicitly repudiated. The document was not an *ex cathedra* utterance and so was not officially infallible. But coming from the Pope it could not be disregarded.

The Vatican Council

PHILIP SCHAFF

Still one of the best brief accounts of the Vatican Council is that by the Rev. Philip Schaff which received wide distribution when it was published in 1875 along with Gladstone's famous pamphlet on "The Vatican Decrees in their Bearing on Civil Allegiance." Schaff was an American theologian and church historian of Swiss extraction. In 1843 he became Professor at the German Reformed Theological Seminary at Mercersburg, Pennsylvania, and from 1870 to 1893 served as Professor at Union Theological Seminary. He was a prolific writer on church history.

MORE than three hundred years after the close of the Council of Trent, Pope Pius IX., who had proclaimed the new dogma of the Immaculate Conception, who in the presence of five hundred Bishops had celebrated the eighteenth centennial of the martyrdom of the Apostles Peter and Paul, and who was permitted to survive not only the golden wedding of his priesthood, but even — alone among his more than two hundred and fifty predecessors — the silver wedding of his popedom (thus falsifying the tradition 'non videbit annos Petri'), resolved to convoke a new oecumenical Council, which was to proclaim his own infallibility in all matters of faith and discipline, and thus to put the top-stone to the pyramid of the Roman hierarchy.

He first intimated his intention, June 26, 1867, in an Allocution to five hundred Bishops who were assembled at the eighteenth centenary of the martyrdom of St. Peter in Rome. The Bishops, in a most humble and obsequious response, July 1, 1867, approved of his heroic courage, to employ, in his old age, an extreme measure for an extreme danger, and predicted a new splendor of the Church, and a new triumph of the kingdom of God. Whereupon the Pope announced to them that he would convene the Council under the special auspices of the Immaculate Virgin, who had crushed the serpent's head and was mighty to destroy alone all the heresies of the world.

The call was issued by an Encyclical, commencing *AEterni Patris Unigenitus Filius*, in the twenty-third year of his Pontificate, on the feast of St. Peter and Paul, June 29, 1868. It created at once a universal commotion in the Christian world, and called forth a multitude of books and pamphlets even before the Council convened. The highest expectations were suspended by the Pope and his sympathizers on the coming event. What the Council of Trent had effected against the Protestant Reformation of the sixteenth century, the Council of the Vatican was to accomplish against the more radical and dangerous foes of modern liberalism and rationalism, which threatened to undermine Romanism itself in its own strongholds. It was to crush the power of infidelity, and to settle all that belongs to the doctrine, worship, and discipline of the Church, and the eternal salvation of souls. It was even hoped

From Philip Schaff, "A History of the Vatican Council" as given in Gladstone and Schaff, *The Vatican Decrees*, pp. 55–79.

that the Council might become a general feast of reconciliation of divided Christendom; and hence the Greek schismatics, and the Protestant heretics and other non-Catholics, were invited by two special letters of the Pope (Sept. 8, and Sept. 13, 1868) to return on this auspicious occasion to 'the only sheepfold of Christ,' for the salvation of their souls.

But the Eastern Patriarchs spurned the invitation, as an insult to their time-honored rights and traditions, from which they could not depart. The Protestant communions either ignored or respectfully declined it.

Thus the Vatican Council, like that of Trent, turned out to be simply a general Roman Council, and apparently put the prospect of a reunion of Christendom farther off than ever before.

While these sanguine expectations of Pius IX. were doomed to disappointment, the chief object of the Council was attained in spite of the strong opposition of the minority of liberal Catholics. This object, which for reasons of propriety is omitted in the bull of convocation and other preliminary acts, but clearly stated by the organs of the Ultramontane or Jesuitical party, was nothing less than the proclamation of the personal *Infallibility of the Pope,* as a binding article of the Roman Catholic faith for all time to come. Herein lies the whole importance of the Council; all the rest dwindles into insignificance, and could never have justified its convocation.

After extensive and careful preparations, the first (and perhaps the last) Vatican Council was solemnly opened amid the sound of innumerable bells and the cannon of St. Angelo, but under frowning skies and a pouring rain, on the festival of the Immaculate Conception of the Virgin Mary, Dec. 8, 1869, in the Basilica of the Vatican. It reached its height at the fourth public session, July 18, 1870, when the decree of Papal Infallibility was proclaimed. After this it dragged on a sickly existence till October 20, 1870, when it was adjourned till Nov. 11, 1870, but indefinitely postponed on account of the extraordinary change in the political situation of Europe. For on the second of September the French Empire, which had been the main support of the temporal power of the Pope, collapsed with the surrender of Napoleon III., at the old Huguenot stronghold of Sedan, to the Protestant King William of Prussia, and on the twentieth of September the Italian troops, in the name of King Victor Emanuel, took possession of Rome, as the future capital of united Italy. . . .

Among the many nations represented, the Italians had a vast majority of 276, of whom 143 belonged to the former Papal States alone. France, with a much larger Catholic population, had only 84, Austria and Hungary 48, Spain 41, Great Britain 35, Germany 19, the United States 48, Mexico 10, Switzerland 8, Belgium 6, Holland 4, Portugal 2, Russia 1. The disproportion between the representatives of the different nations and the number of their constituents was overwhelmingly in favor of the Papal influence. . . .

The subject-matter for deliberation was divided into four parts: on Faith, Discipline, Religious Orders, and on Rites, including Missions. Each part was assigned to a special Commission (*Congregatio* or *Deputatio*), consisting of 24 Prelates elected by ballot for the whole period of the Council, with a presiding Cardinal appointed by the Pope. These Commissions prepared the decrees on the basis of *schemata* previously drawn up by learned divines and canonists, and confidentially submitted to the Bishops in print. The decrees were then discussed, revised, and adopted in secret sessions by the General Congregation (*Congregationes generales*), including all the Fathers, with five presiding Cardinals appointed by the Pope. The General Congregation held eighty-nine sessions in all. Finally, the decrees thus matured were voted upon by simple *yeas* or *nays* (*Placet* or *Non Placet*), and solemnly promulgated in public sessions in the presence and by the authority of the Pope. A conditional assent (*Placet juxta modum*) was allowed in the secret, but not in the public sessions.

There were only four such public sessions held during the ten months of the Council, viz., the opening session (lasting nearly seven hours), Dec. 8, 1869, which was a mere formality, but of a ritualistic splendor and magnificence such as can be gotten up nowhere on earth but in St. Peter's Cathedral in Rome; the second session, Jan. 6, 1870, when the Fathers simply professed each one before the Pope the Nicene Creed and the Profession of the Tridentine Faith; the third session, April 24, 1870, when the dogmatic constitution on the Catholic faith was unanimously adopted; and the fourth session, July 18, 1870, when the first dogmatic constitution on the Church of Christ and the Infallibility of the Pope was adopted with two dissenting votes.

The management of the Council was entirely in the hands of the Pope and his dependent Cardinals and Jesuitical advisers. He originated the topics which were to be acted on; he selected the preparatory committees of theologians (mostly of the Ultramontane school) who, during the winter of 1868–69, drew up the *schemata*; he appointed the presiding officers of the four Deputations, and of the General Congregation; and he proclaimed the decrees in his own name, 'with the approval of the Council.' . . .

More than one hundred Prelates of all nations signed a strong protest (dated Rome, March 1, 1870) against the order of business, especially against the mere majority vote, and expressed the fear that in the end the authority of this Council might be impaired as wanting in truth and liberty — a calamity so direful in these uneasy times, that a greater could not be imagined. But this protest, like all the acts of the minority, was ignored.

The proceedings were, of course, in the official language of the Roman Church, which all Prelates could understand and speak, but very few with sufficient ease to do justice to themselves and their subjects. The acoustic defects of the Council-hall and the difference of pronunciation proved a great inconvenience, and the Continentals complained that they could not understand the English Latin. The Council had a full share of ignorance and superstition, and was disgraced by intrigues and occasional outbursts of intolerance and passion such as are, alas! not unusual in deliberative assemblies even of the Christian Church. But it embraced also much learning and eloquence, especially on the part of the French and German Episcopate. Upon the whole, it compares favorably, as to intellectual ability, moral character, and far-reaching effect, with preceding Roman Councils, and must be regarded as the greatest event in the history of the Papacy since the Council of Trent.

The chief importance of the Council of the Vatican lies in its decree on Papal supremacy and Infallibility. It settled the internal dissensions between Ultramontanism and Gallicanism, which struck at the root of the fundamental principle of authority; it destroyed the independence of the Episcopate, and made it a tool of the Primacy; it crushed liberal Catholicism; it completed the system of Papal absolutism; it raised the hitherto disputed opinion of Papal infallibility to the dignity of a binding article of faith, which no Catholic can deny without loss of salvation. The Pope may now say not only, 'I am the tradition' (*La tradizione son' io*), but also, 'I am the Church' (*L'église c'est moi*)! . . .

In its present form, the Constitution on the Catholic faith is reduced to four chapters, with a proemium and a conclusion. Chap. I. treats of God as the Creator; Chap. II. of revelation; Chap. III. of faith; Chap. IV. of faith and reason. Then follow 18 canons, in which the errors of Pantheism, Naturalism, and Rationalism are condemned in a manner substantially the same, though more clearly and fully, than had been done in the first two sections of the Syllabus. . . .

The preamble, even in its present modified form, derives modern Rationalism and infidelity, as a legitimate fruit, from the heresies condemned by the Council of Trent — that is, from the Protestant Reformation. . . . The boldest testimony heard in the Council was directed against this preamble by Bishop Strossmayer, from the Turkish frontier (March 22, 1870). He characterized the charge against Protestantism as neither just nor charitable. Protestants, he said, abhorred the errors condemned in the schema as much as Catholics. The germ of Rationalism existed in the Catholic Church before the Reformation, especially in the humanism which was nourished in the very sanctuary by the highest dignitaries, and bore its worst fruits in the midst of a Catholic nation at the time of Voltaire and the Encyclopedists. Catholics had produced no better refutation of the errors enumerated in the schema than such men as Leibnitz and Guizot. There were multitudes of Protestants in Germany, England, and North America who loved our Lord Jesus Christ, and had inherited from the shipwreck of faith positive truths and monuments of divine grace. Although this speech was greeted with execrations, it had at least the effect that the objectionable preamble was somewhat modified.

The supplement of the decree binds all Catholics to observe also those constitutions and decrees by which such erroneous opinions as are not here specifically enumerated have been proscribed and condemned by the Holy See. This can be so construed as to include all the eighty errors of the Syllabus. The minority who in the General Congregation had voted *Non Placet* or only a conditional *Placet,* were quieted by the official assurance that the addition involved no new dogma, and had a disciplinary rather than a didactic character. 'Some gave their votes with a heavy heart, conscious of the snare.' Strossmayer

stayed away. Thus a unanimous vote of 667 or 668 fathers was secured in the public session, and the Infallibility decree was virtually anticipated. . . .

The First Dogmatic Constitution on the Church of Christ . . . was passed, with two dissenting votes, in the fourth public session, July 18, 1870. It treats, in four chapters — (1) on the institution of the Apostolic Primacy in the blessed Peter; (2) on the perpetuity of St. Peter's Primacy in the Roman Pontiff; (3) on the power and nature of the Primacy of the Roman Pontiff; (4) on the Infallibility of the Roman Pontiff.

The new features are contained in the last two chapters, which teach *Papal Absolutism* and *Papal Infallibility.* The third chapter vindicates to the Roman Pontiff a superiority of *ordinary* episcopal (not simply an extraordinary primatial) power over all other Churches, and an *immediate* jurisdiction, to which all Catholics, both pastors and people, are bound to submit in matters not only of faith and morals, but even of discipline and government. He is, therefore, the Bishop of Bishops, over every single Bishop, and over all Bishops put together; he is in the fullest sense the Vicar of Christ, and all Bishops are simply Vicars of the Pope. The fourth chapter teaches and defines, as a divinely revealed dogma, that the Roman Pontiff, when speaking from his chair (*ex cathedra*), i.e., in his official capacity, to the Christian world on subjects relating to faith or morals, is infallible, and that such definitions are irreformable (i.e., final and irreversible) in and of themselves, and not in consequence of the consent of the Church.

To appreciate the value and bearing of this decree, we must give a brief history of it.

The Infallibility question was suspended over the Council from the very beginning as the question of questions, for good or for evil. The original plan of the Infallibilists, to decide it by acclamation, had to be abandoned in view of a formidable opposition, which was developed inside and outside of the Council. The majority of the Bishops circulated, early in January, a monster petition, signed by 410 names, in favor of Infallibility. The Italians and the Spaniards circulated similar petitions separately. Archbishop Spalding, of Baltimore, formerly an anti-Infallibilist, prepared an address offering some compromise to the effect that an appeal from the Pope to an œcumenical Council should be reproved. But five counter-petitions, signed by very weighty names, in all, 137, representing various degrees of opposition, but agreed as to the *inopportunity* of the definition, were sent in during the same month (Jan. 12 to 18) by German and Austrian, Hungarian, French, American, Oriental, and Italian Bishops.

The Pope received none of these addresses, but referred them to the Deputation on Faith. While in this he showed his impartiality, he did not conceal, in a private way, his real opinion, and gave it the weight of his personal character and influence. 'Faith in his personal infallibility,' says a well-informed Catholic, 'and belief in a constant and special communication with the Holy Ghost, form the basis of the character of Pius IX.' In the Council itself, Archbishop Manning, the Anglican convert, was the most zealous, devout, and enthusiastic Infallibilist; he urged the definition as the surest means of gaining hesitating Anglo-Catholics and Ritualists longing for *absolute* authority; while his former teacher and friend, Dr. Pusey, feared that the new dogma would make the breach between Oxford and Rome wider than ever. Manning is 'more Catholic than Catholics' to the manor born, as the English settlers in Ireland were more Irish than Irishmen, and is altogether worthy to be the successor of Pius IX in the chair of St. Peter. Both these eminent and remarkable persons show how a sincere faith in a dogma, which borders on blasphemy, may, by a strange delusion or hallucina-

tion, be combined with rare purity and amiability of character.

Besides the all-powerful aid of the Pope, whom no Bishop can disobey without fatal consequences, the Infallibilists had the great advantage of perfect unity of sentiment and aim; while the anti-Infallibilists were divided among themselves, many of them being simply *inopportunists*. They professed to agree with the majority in principle or practice, and to differ from them only on the subordinate question of definability and opportunity. This qualified opposition had no weight whatever with the Pope, who was as fully convinced of the opportunity and necessity of the definition as he was of the dogma itself. And even the most advanced anti-Infallibilists, as Kenrick, Hefele, and Strossmayer, were too much hampered by Romish traditionalism to plant their foot firmly on the Scriptures, which after all must decide all questions of faith.

In the mean time a literary war on Infallibility was carried on in the Catholic Church in Germany, France, and England, and added to the commotion in Rome. A large number of pamphlets, written or inspired by prominent members of the Council, appeared for and against Infallibility. Distinguished outsiders, as Döllinger, Gratry, Hyacinthe, Montalembert, and Newman, mixed in the fight, and strengthened the minority. . . .

After preliminary skirmishes, the formal discussion began in earnest in the 50th session of the General Congregation, May 13, 1870, and lasted to the 86th General Congregation, July 16. About eighty Latin speeches were delivered in the general discussion on the schema *de Romano Pontifice*, nearly one half of them on the part of the opposition, which embraced less than one fifth of the Council. When the arguments and the patience of the assembly were pretty well exhausted, the President, at the petition of a hundred and fifty Bishops, closed the general discussion on the third day of June. About forty more Bishops, who had entered their names, were thus prevented from speaking; but one of them, Archbishop Kenrick, of St. Louis, published his strong argument against Infallibility in Naples. Then five special discussions commenced on the proemium and the four chapters. 'For the fifth or last discussion a hundred and twenty Bishops inscribed their names to speak; fifty of them were heard, until on both sides the burden became too heavy to bear; and, by mutual consent, a useless and endless discussion, from mere exhaustion, ceased.'

When the vote was taken on the whole four chapters of the Constitution of the Church, July 13, 1870, in the 85th secret session of the General Congregation (601 members being present), 451 voted *Placet*, 88 *Non Placet*, 62 *Placet juxta modum*, over 80 (perhaps 91), though present in Rome or in the neighborhood, abstained for various reasons from voting. Among the negative votes were the Prelates most distinguished for learning and position, as SCHWARZENBERG, Cardinal Prince-Archbishop of Prague; RAUSCHER, Cardinal Prince-Archbishop of Vienna; DARBOY, Archbishop of Paris; MATTHIEU, Cardinal-Archbishop of Besançon; GINOULHIAC, Archbishop of Lyons; DUPANLOUP, Bishop of Orleans; MARET, Bishop of Sura (i. p.); SIMOR, Archbishop of Gran and Primate of Hungary; HAYNALD, Archbishop of Kalocsa; FÖRSTER, Prince-Archbishop of Breslau; SCHERR, Archbishop of Munich; KETTELER, Bishop of Mayence; HEFELE, Bishop of Rottenburg; STROSSMAYER, Bishop of Bosnia and Sirmium; MACHALE, Archbishop of Tuam; CONNOLLY, Archbishop of Halifax; KENRICK, Archbishop of St. Louis.

On the evening of the 13th of July the minority sent a deputation, consisting of Simor, Ginoulhiac, Scherr, Darboy, Ketteler, and Rivet, to the Pope. After waiting an hour, they were admitted at 9 o'clock in the evening. They asked simply for a withdrawal of the addition to the third chapter, which assigns to the Pope the exclusive possession of all ecclesiastical powers, and for the insertion, in the fourth chapter, of a clause limiting his infallibility to those decisions which he pronounces '*innixus testimonio ecclesiarum* [relying on the witness of the churches]' Pius returned the almost incredible answer: 'I shall do what I can, my dear sons, but I have not yet read the scheme; I do not know what it contains.' He requested Darboy, the spokesman of the deputation, to hand him the petition in writing. Darboy promised to do so; and added, not without irony, that he would send with it the schema which the Deputation on Faith and the Legates had with such culpable levity omitted to lay before his Holiness, exposing him to the risk of proclaiming in a few days a decree he was ignorant of. Pius surprised the deputation by the astounding assurance that the whole Church had always taught the unconditional Infallibility of the Pope. Then Bishop Ketteler of Mayence implored the Holy Father on his knees to make some concession for the peace and unity of the Church. This prostration of the proudest of the German prelates made some impression. Pius dismissed the deputation in a hopeful temper. But immediately afterwards Manning and Senestrey (Bishop of Regensburg) strengthened his faith, and frightened him by the warning that, if he made any concession, he would be disgraced in history as a second Honorius.

In the secret session on the 16th of July, on motion of some Spanish Bishops, an addition was inserted '*non autem ex consensu ecclesiae* [and not from the consent of the church],' which makes the decree still more obnoxious. On the same day Cardinal Rauscher, in a private audience, made another attempt to induce the Pope to yield, but was told, 'It is too late.'

On the 17th of July fifty-six Bishops sent a written protest to the Pope, declaring that nothing had occurred to change their conviction as expressed in their negative vote; on the contrary, they were confirmed in it; yet filial piety and reverence for the Holy Father would not permit them to vote *Non Placet* openly and in his face, in a matter which so intimately concerned his person, and that therefore they had resolved to return forthwith to their flocks, which had already too long been deprived of their presence, and were now filled with apprehensions of war. Schwarzenberg, Matthieu, Simor, and Darboy head the list of signers. On the evening of the same day not only the fifty-six signers, but sixty additional members of the opposition departed from Rome, promising to each other to make their future conduct dependent on mutual understanding.

This was the turning-point: the opposition broke down by its own act of cowardice. They ought to have stood like men on the post of duty, and repeated their negative vote according to their honest convictions. They could thus have prevented the passage of this momentous decree, or at all events shorn it of its oecumenical weight, and kept it open for future revision and possible reversal. But they left Rome at the very moment when their presence was most needed, and threw an easy victory into the lap of the majority.

When, therefore, the fourth public session was held, on the memorable 18th of July (Monday), there were but 535 Fathers present, and of these all voted *Placet*, with the exception of two, viz., Bishop Riccio, of Cajazzo, in Sicily, and Bishop Fitzgerald, of Little Rock, Arkansas, who had the courage to vote *Non Placet*, but immediately, before the close of the session, submitted to the voice of the Council. In this way a moral unanimity was secured as great as in the first Council of Nicaea, where likewise two refused to subscribe to the Nicene Creed. 'What a wise direction of Providence,' exclaimed the *Civiltà cattolica*, '535 yeas against 2 nays. *Only two* nays, therefore almost total unanimity; and yet two *nays*, therefore full liberty of the Council. How vain are all attacks against the oecumenical character of this most beautiful of all Councils!'

After the vote the Pope confirmed the decrees and canons on the Constitution of the Church of Christ, and added from his own inspiration the assurance that the supreme authority of the Roman Pontiff did not suppress but aid, not destroy but build up, and formed the best protection of the rights and interests of the Episcopate.

The days of the two most important public sessions of the Vatican Council, namely the first and the last, were the darkest and stormiest which Rome saw from Dec. 8, 1869 to the 18th of July, 1870. The Episcopal votes and the Papal proclamation of the new dogma were accompanied by flashes of lightning and claps of thunder from the skies, and so great was the darkness which spread over the Church of St. Peter, that the Pope could not read the decree of his own Infallibility without the artificial light of a candle. This voice of nature was variously interpreted, either as a condemnation of Gallicanism and liberal Catholicism, or as a divine attestation of the dogma like that which accompanied the promulgation of the law from Mount Sinai, or as an evil omen of impending calamities to the Papacy. . . .

What did the Bishops of the minority do? They all submitted, even those who had been most vigorous in opposing, not only the opportunity of the definition, but the dogma itself. Some hesitated long, but yielded at last to the heavy pressure. . . .

The Powers and the Vatican Council

Rumors that the dogma of Papal Infallibility would be proclaimed at the forthcoming Vatican Council alarmed the chancelleries of Europe and Prince Hohenlohe, the Prime Minister of Bavaria, attempted in the spring of 1869 to bring about concerted action by the powers. His famous note (to be found in Hohenlohe, *Memoirs*, I, 326) is discussed by Lord Acton, noted English liberal Catholic historian and opponent of infallibility. Acton was a friend of Gladstone and of Professor Döllinger of Munich, and late in life as Regius Professor of Modern History at Cambridge planned the many volumed *Cambridge Modern History*. The general position of the powers during the Council is succinctly summarized by an American scholar and Professor of History at Meredith College, Dr. Lillian Parker Wallace.

The Bavarian Proposal

LORD ACTON

It happened that a statesman was in office who had occasion to know that the information [about the intention to announce the proclamation of papal infallibility] was accurate. The Prime Minister of Bavaria, Prince Hohenlohe, was the brother of a cardinal; the University of Munich was represented on the Roman commissions by an illustrious scholar; and the news of the thing that was preparing came through trustworthy channels. On the 9th of April [1869] Prince Hohenlohe sent out a diplomatic circular on the subject of the Council. He pointed out that it was not called into existence by any purely theological emergency, and that the one dogma which was to be brought before it involved all those claims which cause collisions between Church and State, and threaten the liberty and the security of governments. Of the five Roman Commissions, one was appointed for the express purpose of dealing with the mixed topics common to religion and to politics. Be-

sides infallibility and politics, the Council was to be occupied with the Syllabus, which is in part directed against maxims of State. The avowed purpose of the Council being so largely political, the governments could not remain indifferent to its action. Lest they should be driven afterwards to adopt measures which would be hostile, it would be better at once to seek an understanding by friendly means, and to obtain assurance that all irritating deliberations should be avoided, and no business touching the State transacted except in presence of its representatives. He proposed that the governments should hold a conference to arrange a plan for the protection of their common interest.

Important measures proposed by small States are subject to suspicion of being prompted by a greater power. Prince Hohenlohe, as a friend of the Prussian alliance, was supposed to be acting in this matter in concert with Berlin. This good understanding was suspected at Vienna;

From Lord Acton, "The Vatican Council" in *North British Review*, LIII (1870), pp. 99–100.

for the Austrian Chancellor was more conspicuous as an enemy of Prussia than Hohenlohe as a friend. Count Beust traced the influence of Count Bismarck in the Bavarian circular. He replied, in behalf of the Catholic empire of Austria, that there were no grounds to impute political objects to the Council, and that repression and not prevention was the only policy compatible with free institutions. After the refusal of Austria, the idea of a conference was dismissed by the other powers; and the first of the storm clouds that darkened the horizon of infallibility passed without breaking.

Fruitless Efforts toward Concerted Action

LILLIAN PARKER WALLACE

THE consensus of opinion among the powers was that the decisions of the Council should be left to the Council. They trusted the minority to make a determined stand against anything which might endanger the interests of the state. The minority bishops on the other hand were coming to the conclusion that nothing but intervention on the part of the civil governments would be of any avail. One hundred bishops signed a protest against the *schema de ecclesia*. The protest was ignored. Darboy [Archbishop of Paris] rather sadly exclaimed that to lay protests before His Holiness was fruitless, no answers being forthcoming. Nothing but a direct appeal to the governments could assure the freedom of the bishops.

On March 6 [1870] the dogma of Infallibility was laid before the fathers and six days later it was proposed that it be discussed at once *extra ordinem*. The immediate action of Daru [French foreign minister] was to telegraph to Rome asking that no decision be taken (it had been announced for March 17) without waiting for the arrival of the French representative.

Italy, meanwhile, had raised the question of a concerted *démarche* and had attempted to sound out Beust [of Austria-Hungary] on the matter. Beust was not favorably inclined to the idea of having a representative at the Council. Such a representative would be confronted constantly by the alternative of irritating the Council and the Pope or being criticised by his government for weakness and failure. Furthermore, Beust was unwilling to make common cause with the minority and later have to swallow everything they had agreed to. Nevertheless he was sympathetic with Daru's desire to intervene effectively and instructed his representative in Rome to try to prevail on the Roman court to take the French demand under consideration and not make a precipitous decision without hearing the French objections.

Among the majority in Rome the action of Daru was regarded as an attempt to intimidate the Holy Father. Arnim, the Prussian Ambassador, would have been glad to support Daru's proposed intervention. He was growing increasingly pessimistic over the ability of the minority to defend their point of view without support from the civil governments. Bismarck, however, persisted in his refusal to intervene. In the eyes of the Curia Prussia was the foremost Protestant power and should not interfere in questions within the province of the Catholic Church. Italy, too, felt that under the circumstances

From Lillian Parker Wallace, *The Papacy and European Diplomacy, 1869–1878* (Chapel Hill: The University of North Carolina Press, 1948), pp. 91–94, 96–101. Reprinted by permission of the publisher.

it would be too difficult to send a representative and agreed that France was the state to undertake the move, whatever it might be.

Daru's proposal to send a special envoy did not meet with [Premier] Ollivier's approval. If the French Ambassador, Banneville, was not all right he should be replaced. If there was no objection to him, let him handle the protest. A memorandum should be sent to him to lay before the Council after which he should withdraw in dignity.

Antonelli, the Cardinal Secretary of State, in replying to the mild remonstrance which the French cabinet had permitted Daru to send under the date of February 20, attempted to allay the suspicions and fears of the French Foreign Minister. He expressed the gratitude of the Holy See for the protection afforded for twenty years by the French troops. He expressed astonishment that declarations made in the *Augsburger Zeitung,* in violation of pontifical secrecy could have made so profound an impression on the French cabinet as to cause them to alter their policy with reference to the freedom of the Council. He expressly stated that the Church had no intention of exercising any direct and absolute power over the political rights of the State and denied that the definition of Infallibility would in any way change the relations between the bishops and the Pope. He voiced the hope that in view of these explanations the French government would not insist on intervention as suggested in Daru's dispatch.

The question before France was whether to accept Antonelli's explanations or to insist upon intervention as the minority requested. Banneville was summoned home for consultation. The two parties in the Council were squarely opposed to each other. The majority insisted that there was no cause for alarm on the part of the civil government. The minority, on the other hand, maintained that the Council was not free, that the Church was on the point of altering itself so that the Church with

which the French concordat was signed would no longer exist, and that the controversy was not a purely dogmatic one but that the peace and quiet of the nation was at stake. The decision eventually reached on Daru's insistence was that a memorandum should be sent to the Pope who was to lay it before the Council. The memorandum was not to concern itself with the question of Infallibility but simply with the *schema de ecclesia.* The majority of the cabinet would have preferred to consider the question closed. The other cabinets of Europe were invited to support this *démarche.*

Daru's memorandum was prepared on April 5 but was not to be presented for another fortnight. The proposal to send a special ambassador had received no support from the other cabinets of Europe and, except for Daru, the French cabinet had likewise rejected this idea. Consequently the memorandum was to wait until the return of Banneville to Rome or the appointment of a new French ambassador. . . . The decision finally reached was that Banneville was to continue as ambassador to the Holy See and that he should be the one to present the memorandum. The ministers of Austria, Bavaria, and Prussia had been instructed to support this step. The ambassadors of Spain and Portugal together with Odo Russell of England had likewise been instructed to adhere.

Banneville returned to Rome on April 14 and on the following day presented the memorandum to Antonelli for the Pope's consideration before the formal audience, which was to be granted on April 22. Much was expected of the protest from France as it was couched in stronger terms than the mild remonstrance of February. The prospect of state interference was a subject of intense interest to all who were directly participating in conciliar affairs and also to many observers who were vitally concerned. The general change in atmosphere, the greater confidence of the minority were commented on by Russell in one of his reports to Manning [Archbishop of Westminster].

The memorandum referred to the dispatch of February 20 as explaining why the French government decided to depart from its previous attitude of abstention and reiterated the declarations of that note against subordinating the State to the Church. All intentions to intervene in spiritual matters were disclaimed. As evidence of this point was cited the Emperor's refusal to exercise his right of sending a special representative to the Council, a right always held by the crown of France and never contested by a pope. Questions of civil and political order having been brought up, however, it had become necessary for the French government to let its position be known. There was no intention of putting pressure on the deliberations of the Council. The intervention was purely moral and limited to matters indisputably belonging to the civil power. The Pope and the fathers were asked to set aside everything in the *schema de ecclesia* which could have disastrous consequences on the legal and social order of all the states of Europe. "The more one examines, indeed, the doctrine summed up in this document the less is it possible to ignore that this doctrine, fundamentally, is equivalent to the complete subordination of civil society to religious society." Either more plausible explanations or modifications were asked for. It seemed that the "*schema de ecclesia* had as its aim and object to reestablish in the whole world the ascendancy of doctrines subordinating civil society to the empire of the clergy." The infallibility and authority would have only such limits as the Church might assign. The most fundamental rights of property, family and education could be called in question. Power would not only be concentrated in the Church but ecclesiastical power would be concentrated in its head.

Copies of this memorandum were sent simultaneously by Daru to all the chancelleries of Europe. From some one of these chancelleries, either advertently or inadvertently, a copy of the memorandum came into the possession of the *Augsburger Zeitung* and was published before the Pope received Banneville. His Holiness was much hurt at what he considered an act of disrespect but received the French explanation that it had been a mistake for which they were not responsible.

In the meantime, after the memorandum had been sent to Rome and before it had been handed to Antonelli for the Pope's perusal, Daru had suddenly resigned. The news was telegraphed to Rome in the following words: "Daru resigns. Ollivier takes his place. Council free." Ollivier had, indeed, taken over the portfolio of the Foreign Minister. The Infallibilists in Rome were much heartened by this turn of events which removed a very powerful opponent from a position of authority. Ollivier might have recalled the memorandum as there was still time, but he refused to do so. Nevertheless he was determined not to press the matter further.

Because of the religious ceremonies of Holy Week, Banneville's audience with the Pope had been delayed until April 22 although the latter had had the memorandum for perusal since April 15. Banneville presented the document formally in a very respectful manner with the request that it be conveyed by the Pope to the Council. This the Pope declined to do. Most of Banneville's colleagues supported this *démarche* orally, but Arnim, the Prussian Ambassador, wrote a note couched in stronger terms than the memorandum. By implication he condemned, not only the sections of the *schema de ecclesia* which were the subject of Daru's memorandum, but even "changes introduced in the delimitation of the authority attributed to each degree of the hierarchy," that is, the definition of the dogma of Infallibility.

Antonelli's reply to the collective *démarche* of the European countries was evasive. He said the texts presented to the Council were not definitive but capable of modification and amendment, for merely the preparatory work was done. In general he simply amplified or reiterated the statements he had made in his reply to the

French note of February 20. Bishop Ullathorne, writing to a friend in England who undertook to show the letter to Gladstone, made precisely the same point, that the *schema* was in each case merely a point of departure and would be modified in almost every particular by the fathers when they had an opportunity to discuss it.

The minority party in Rome was now full of hope. They counted 150 among their members, including thirty-four French, forty-seven Germans, and twenty Italians. The International Committee was meeting every afternoon. New adherents were being added. They had been delighted by the French memorandum and felt that their position was so strengthened that they were confident of success and expected to bring about the adjournment of the Council *sine die* without any definition of Infallibility. There was no occasion, however, for rejoicing. The possibility of accomplishing anything through the intervention of the civil governments had been ended by Daru's resignation. The civil governments, led by France, resumed the role of simple observers. The action of the cabinets had exercised no positive effect on the deliberations of the Council. It had, however, to some extent bolstered up the minority. In the meanwhile, however, between Banneville's arrival in Rome and his audience with the Pope it was decided to alter the regular order of business in the Council and proceed at once to the discussion of the *schema de ecclesia*. The preface and first four chapters were unanimously adopted on April 24, receiving 667 votes. The preamble which had aroused the wrath of Strossmayer in the stormy session of March 22 and the indignation of Prussia when it was reported by Arnim had been changed and softened so that the minority bishops gave their assent. They were somewhat dubious about a final phrase, however, that was appended at the last moment which seemed in itself to be a sort of statement of personal papal Infallibility. When assured that the phrase was purely rhetorical and had no dogmatic

significance whatever, they reluctantly assented. It was not until later that they realized they had given their assent unwittingly to the dogma they were pledged to resist.

The ground was now cleared for proceeding to the question of Infallibility. The turning point for the minority, however, had already been reached. While the collective *démarche* led by France had been in sight the minority had been strengthened. Now, little by little, they began to lose ground. The Archbishop of Paris reported to Emperor Napoleon III on May 2 that they were still holding firm but had lost some members by death and some by departure from the Council. The only diplomatic representative in Rome who was actively bestirring himself in support of the minority was Arnim, the Prussian Ambassador, whose hands were partially tied by Bismarck's instructions not to intervene. Arnim was convinced that the definition of Infallibility would be highly dangerous to Europe. As he expressed it later in a letter to Döllinger, it was not "merely a precious vase, designed to adorn the Vatican, but a Pandora box from which one might spread, should the occasion arise, ingredients dangerous to the Catholic world." The discussion began on May 13 but did not reach a crucial stage until May 25. Darboy wrote again to the Emperor on May 21 hoping that the minority might yet receive enough support to be able to prevent the definition. He spoke of the memorandum which had been presented by Banneville and had been ignored and of Banneville's instructions from Ollivier (still holding the portfolio of foreign affairs until Gramont could be recalled from Vienna to assume the office) to maintain a strictly "hands-off" policy, merely reporting events as they occurred but doing nothing to shape them. He suggested recalling Banneville and said it would help the minority. He still thought there was time if action were not further delayed. The request was refused. The affairs of the Council proceeded unhampered by any interference from the outside.

The Vatican Decrees: Selections

In its third public session the Vatican Council on April 24, 1870, published the Dogmatic Constitution of the Catholic Faith. In its fourth public session on July 18, 1870, the Vatican Council published the First Dogmatic Constitution of the Church of Christ. An introductory statement was followed by four chapters: I, Of the Institution of the Apostolic Primacy in blessed Peter; II, On the Perpetuity of the Primacy of blessed Peter in the Roman Pontiffs; III, On the Power and the Nature of the Primacy of the Roman Pontiff; IV, Concerning the Infallible Teaching of the Roman Pontiff. As their titles indicate, the first two chapters are primarily historical in character and are here omitted. Chapters III and IV which define the power of the Pope and the obedience due him are pertinent to the problem of church and state in the period after 1870 and excerpts from these are quoted.

Chapter III: On the Power and Nature of the Primacy of the Roman Pontiff

Wherefore, resting on plain testimonies of the Sacred Writings, and adhering to the plain and express decrees both of our predecessors, the Roman Pontiffs, and of the General Councils we renew the definition of the oecumenical Council of Florence, in virtue of which all the faithful of Christ must believe that the holy Apostolic See and the Roman Pontiff possesses the primacy over the whole world, and that the Roman Pontiff is the successor of blessed Peter, Prince of the Apostles, and is true vicar of Christ, and head of the whole Church, and father and teacher of all Christians; and that full power was given to him in blessed Peter to rule, feed, and govern the universal Church by Jesus Christ our Lord; as is also contained in the acts of the General Councils and in the sacred Canons.

Hence we teach and declare that by the appointment of our Lord the Roman Church possesses a superiority of ordinary power over all other churches, and that this power of jurisdiction of the Roman Pontiff, which is truly episcopal, is immediate; to which all, of whatever rite and dignity, both pastors and faithful, both individually and collectively, are bound, by their duty of hierarchical subordination and true obedience, to submit not only in matters which belong to faith and morals, but also in those that appertain to the discipline and government of the Church throughout the world, so that the Church of Christ may be one flock under one supreme pastor through the preservation of unity both of communion and of profession of the same faith with the Roman Pontiff. This is the teaching of Catholic truth, from which no one can deviate without loss of faith and of salvation. . . .

Further, from this supreme power possessed by the Roman Pontiff of governing the universal Church, it follows that he has the right of free communication with the pastors of the whole Church, and with their flocks, that these may be taught and ruled by him in the way of salvation. Wherefore we condemn and reject the opinions of those who hold that the communication between this supreme head and the pastors and their flocks can lawfully be impeded; or who make this communication subject to the will of the secular power, so as to maintain that whatever is done by the Apostolic See, or by its authority, for the government of the Church, can not have force or value unless it be

From Gladstone and Schaff, *op. cit.*, pp. 159–168, where both the Latin text and the English translation by Archbishop Manning are given.

confirmed by the assent of the secular power.

And since by the divine right of Apostolic primacy the Roman Pontiff is placed over the universal Church, we further teach and declare that he is the supreme judge of the faithful, and that in all causes, the decision of which belongs to the Church, recourse may be had to his tribunal, and that none may re-open the judgment of the Apostolic See, than whose authority there is no greater, nor can any lawfully review its judgment. Wherefore they err from the right course who assert that it is lawful to appeal from the judgments of the Roman Pontiffs to an oecumenical Council, as to an authority higher than that of the Roman Pontiff.

. If, then, any shall say that the Roman Pontiff has the office merely of inspection or direction, and not full and supreme power of jurisdiction over the universal Church, not only in things which belong to faith and morals, but also in those which relate to the discipline and government of the Church spread throughout the world; or assert that he possesses merely the principal part, and not all the fullness of this supreme power; or that this power which he enjoys is not ordinary and immediate, both over each and all the churches, and over each and all the pastors and the faithful: let him be anathema.

Chapter IV: Concerning the Infallible Teaching of the Roman Pontiff

Moreover, that the supreme power of teaching is also included in the Apostolic primacy, which the Roman Pontiff, as the successor of Peter, Prince of the Apostles, possesses over the whole Church, this Holy See has always held, the perpetual practice of the Church confirms, and oecumenical Councils also have declared, especially those in which the East with the West met in the union of faith and charity. For the Fathers of the Fourth Council of Constantinople, following in the footsteps of their predecessors, gave forth this solemn profession: The first condition of salvation is to keep the rule of the true faith. And because the sentence of our Lord Jesus Christ can not be passed by, who said: 'Thou art Peter, and upon this rock I will build my Church,' these things which have been said are approved by events, because in the Apostolic See the Catholic religion and her holy and well-known doctrine has always been kept undefiled. . . .

This gift, then, of truth and never-failing faith was conferred by heaven upon Peter and his successors in this chair, that they might perform their high office for the salvation of all; that the whole flock of Christ, kept away by them from the poisonous food of error, might be nourished with the pasture of heavenly doctrine; that the occasion of schism being removed, the whole Church might be kept one, and, resting on its foundation, might stand firm against the gates of hell.

But since in this very age, in which the salutary efficacy of the Apostolic office is most of all required, not a few are found who take away from its authority, we judge it altogether necessary solemnly to assert the prerogative which the only begotten Son of God vouchsafed to join with the supreme pastoral office.

Therefore faithfully adhering to the tradition received from the beginning of the Christian faith, for the glory of God our Saviour, the exaltation of the Catholic religion, and the salvation of Christian people, the sacred Council approving, we teach and define that it is a dogma divinely revealed: that the Roman Pontiff, when he speaks *ex cathedra*, that is, when in discharge of the office of pastor and doctor of all Christians, by virtue of his supreme Apostolic authority, he defines a doctrine regarding faith or morals to be held by the universal Church, by the divine assistance promised to him in blessed Peter, is possessed of that infallibility with which the divine Redeemer willed that his Church should be endowed for defining doctrine regarding faith or morals; and that therefore such definitions of the Roman Pontiff are irreformable of themselves, and not from the consent of the Church.

But if any one — which may God avert — presume to contradict this our definition: let him be anathema.

Papal Infallibility: Cause for Alarm?

By all odds the most important and controversial dogma among the Vatican decrees was the one proclaiming Papal Infallibility. Just what did it mean and how would the power be used in the future? What was involved by the phrase "ex cathedra," literally "from the chair," and what constituted "Faith and Morals"? What was the relation of Infallibility to the Syllabus? Churchmen, scholars, statesmen, ordinary people were concerned about these questions. Below are presented selections touching on these topics. The first is an interpretation by Johann J. I. von Döllinger, foremost Catholic theologian and Professor of Ecclesiastical History at the University of Munich, who led the opposition to Papal Infallibility in Germany; the second is by Gladstone whose pamphlet on "The Vatican Decrees," is one of his most famous polemical efforts; the third is an answer to Gladstone by Archbishop Manning, leader of the Ultramontane party in England and a strong supporter of Papal Infallibility; the fourth is a note from the Austrian Foreign Minister Count Beust which is indicative of the fear which swept European chancelleries as a result of the proclamation of Papal Infallibility.

A Liberal Catholic View

JOHANN J. I. VON DÖLLINGER

ONE difficulty resulted from the formulization of the doctrine of Infallibility, for the solution of which a variety of hypotheses have been invented, without any unanimity among theologians in accepting some one of them being secured. Every theologian, on closer inspection, found Papal decisions which contradicted other doctrines laid down by Popes or generally received in the Church, or which appeared to him doubtful; and it seemed impossible to declare all these to be products of an infallible authority. It became necessary, therefore, to specify some distinctive marks by which a really infallible decision of a Pope might be recognized, or to fix certain conditions in the absence of which the pronouncement is not to be regarded as infallible. And thus, since the sixteenth century, there

grew up the famous distinction of Papal decisions promulgated ex cathedrâ, and therefore dogmatically and without any possibility of error.

The distinction between a judgment pronounced ex cathedrâ and a merely occasional or casual utterance is, indeed, a perfectly reasonable one, not only in the case of the Pope, but of any bishop or professor. In other words, every one whose office it is to teach can, and will at times, speak off-hand and loosely on dogmatic and ethical questions, whereas, in his capacity of a public and official teacher, he pronounces deliberately, and with serious regard to the consequences of his teaching. No reasonable man will pretend that the remarks made by a Pope in conversation are definitions of faith. But beyond this the distinction has no meaning. When a

From Janus [Johann J. I. von Döllinger] and others, *The Pope and Council* (Boston: Roberts Brothers, 1870), pp. 327–329.

Pope speaks publicly on a point of doctrine, either of his own accord, or in answer to questions addressed to him, he has spoken *ex cathedrâ,* for he was questioned as Pope, and successor of other Popes, and the mere fact that he has made his declaration publicly and in writing makes it an *ex cathedrâ* judgment. This holds good equally of every bishop. The moment any accidental or arbitrary condition is fixed on which the *ex cathedrâ* nature of a Papal decision is to depend, we enter the sphere of the private crochets of theologians, such as are wont to be devised simply to meet the difficulties of the system. Of such notions, one is as good as another; they come

and go, and are afterwards noted down. It is just as if one chose to say afterwards of a physician who had been consulted, and had given his opinion on a disease, that he had formed his diagnosis or prescribed his remedies as a private person and not as a physician. As soon, therefore, as limitations are introduced, and the dogmatic judgments of the Popes are divided into two classes, the *ex cathedrâ* and the personal ones, it is obvious that the sole ground for this arbitrary distinction lies in the fact that there are sure to be some inconvenient decisions of Popes which it is desirable to except from the privilege of infallibility generally asserted in other cases.

A Threat to the Integrity of Civil Allegiance

W. E. GLADSTONE

WILL it, then, be said that the infallibility of the Pope accrues only when he speaks *ex cathedrâ?* No doubt this is a very material consideration for those who have been told that the private conscience is to derive comfort and assurance from the emanations of the Papal Chair: for there is no established or accepted definition of the phrase *ex cathedrâ,* and he has no power to obtain one, and no guide to direct him in his choice among some twelve theories on the subject, which, it is said, are bandied to and fro among Roman theologians, except the despised and discarded agency of his private judgment. But while thus sorely tantalized, he is not one whit protected. For there is still one person, and one only, who can unquestionably declare *ex cathedrâ* what is *ex cathedrâ* and what is not, and who can declare it when and as he pleases. That person is the Pope himself. The provision is, that no document he issues shall be valid without a seal; but the

seal remains under his own sole lock and key.

Again, it may be sought to plead that the Pope is, after all, only operating by sanctions which unquestionably belong to the religious domain. He does not propose to invade the country, to seize Woolwich or burn Portsmouth. He will only, at the worst, excommunicate opponents, as he has excommunicated Dr. von Döllinger and others. Is this a good answer? After all, even in the Middle Ages, it was not by the direct action of fleets and armies of their own that the Popes contended with kings who were refractory; it was mainly by interdicts, and by the refusal, which they entailed when the Bishops were not brave enough to refuse their publication, of religious offices to the people. It was thus that England suffered under John, France under Philip Augustus; Leon under Alphonso the Noble, and every country in its turn. But the inference may be drawn that they who, while using spiritual weapons

From W. E. Gladstone, "The Vatican Decrees in their Bearing on Civil Allegiance" in Gladstone and Schaff, *op. cit.,* pp. 26–31.

for such an end, do not employ temporal means, only fail to employ them because they have them not. A religious society which delivers volleys of spiritual censure in order to impede the performance of civil duties does all the mischief that is in its power to do, and brings into question, in face of the State, its title to civil protection.

Will it be said, finally, that the Infallibility touches only matter of faith and morals? Only matter of morals! Will any of the Roman casuists kindly acquaint us what are the departments and functions of human life which do not and can not fall within the domain of morals? If they will not tell us, we must look elsewhere. In his work entitled *Literature and Dogma*, Mr. Matthew Arnold quaintly informs us — as they tell us nowadays how many parts of our poor bodies are solid and how many aqueous — that about seventy-five per cent. of all we do belongs to the department of 'conduct.' Conduct and morals, we may suppose, are nearly co-extensive. Three fourths, then, of life are thus 'handed over. But who will guarantee to us the other fourth? Certainly not St. Paul, who says, 'Whether therefore ye eat, or drink, or whatsoever ye do, do *all* to the glory of God.' And, 'Whatsoever ye do, in word or in deed, do *all* in the name of the Lord Jesus.' No! Such a distinction would be the unworthy device of a shallow policy, vainly used to hide the daring of that wild ambition which at Rome, not from the throne, but from behind the throne, prompts the movements of the Vatican. I care not to ask if there be dregs or tatters of human life, such as can escape from the description and boundary of morals. I submit that Duty is a power which rises with us in the morning, and goes to rest with us at night. It is co-extensive with the action of our intelligence. It is the shadow which cleaves to us go where we will, and which only leaves us when we leave the light of life. So, then, it is the supreme direction of us in respect to all Duty which the Pontiff declares to belong to him *sacro approbante concilio* [the sacred council approving]; and this declaration he makes, not as an otiose opinion of the schools, but *cunctis fidelibus credendam et tenendam* [to be believed and held by all the faithful].

But we shall now see that, even if a loophole had at this point been left unclosed, the void is supplied by another provision of the Decrees. While the reach of the Infallibility is as wide as it may please the Pope, or those who may prompt the Pope, to make it, there is something wider still, and that is the claim to an absolute and entire Obedience. This Obedience is to be rendered to his orders in the cases I shall proceed to point out, without any qualifying condition, such as the *ex cathedrâ*. The sounding name of Infallibility has so fascinated the public mind, and riveted it on the Fourth Chapter of the Constitution *de Ecclesiâ*, that its near neighbor, the Third Chapter, has, at least in my opinion, received very much less than justice. Let us turn to it: [At this point, Gladstone quoted a few phrases in Latin; here they are translated and quoted in context, with Gladstone's omissions indicated by parentheses.]

(Hence we teach and declare that by the appointment of our Lord the Roman Church possesses a superiority of ordinary power over all other churches, and that this power of jurisdiction of the Roman Pontiff, which is truly episcopal, is immediate;) to which all, of whatever rite and dignity, both pastors and faithful, both individually and collectively, are bound, by their duty of hierarchical subordination and true obedience, to submit not only in matters which belong to faith and morals, but also in those that appertain to the discipline and government of the Church throughout the world, (so that the Church of Christ may be one flock under one supreme pastor through the preservation of unity both of communion and of profession of the same faith with the Roman Pontiff.) This is the teaching of Catholic truth, from which no one can deviate without loss of faith and of salvation. . . .

(And since by the divine right of Apostolic primacy the Roman Pontiff is placed over the universal Church,) we further teach and declare that he is the supreme judge of the faithful, and that in all causes, the decision of which belongs to the Church, recourse may be had to his tribunal, and that none may re-open the judgment of the Apostolic See, than whose authority there is no greater, nor can any lawfully review its judgment.

Even, therefore, where the judgments of the Pope do not present the credentials of Infallibility, they are unappealable and irreversible; no person may pass judgment upon them; and all men, clerical and lay, dispersedly or in the aggregate, are bound truly to obey them; and from this rule of Catholic truth no man can depart, save at the peril of his salvation. Surely, it is allowable to say that this Third Chapter on universal Obedience is a formidable rival to the Fourth Chapter on Infallibility. Indeed, to an observer from without, it seems to leave the dignity to the other, but to reserve the stringency and efficiency to itself. The Third Chapter is the Merovingian Monarch; the Fourth is the Carolingian Mayor of the Palace. The Third has an overawing splendor; the Fourth, an iron grip. Little does it matter to me whether my superior claims infallibility, so long as he is entitled to demand and exact conformity. This, it will be observed, he demands even in cases not covered by his infallibility; cases, therefore, in which he admits it to be possible that he may be wrong, but finds it intolerable to be told so. As he must be obeyed in all his judgments, though not *ex cathedrâ*, it seems a pity he could not likewise give the comforting assurance that they are all certain to be right.

But why this ostensible reduplication — this apparent surplusage? Why did the astute contrivers of this tangled scheme conclude that they could not afford to rest content with pledging the Council to Infallibility in terms which are not only wide to a high degree, but elastic beyond all measure?

Though they must have known perfectly well that 'faith and morals' carried every thing, or every thing worth having,

in the purely individual sphere, they also knew just as well that, even where the individual was subjugated, they might and would still have to deal with the State.

In mediaeval history, this distinction is not only clear, but glaring. Outside the borders of some narrow and proscribed sect, now and then emerging, we never, or scarcely ever, hear of private and personal resistance to the Pope. The manful 'Protestantism' of mediaeval times had its activity almost entirely in the sphere of public, national, and State rights. Too much attention, in my opinion, can not be fastened on this point. It is the very root and kernel of the matter. Individual servitude, however abject, will not satisfy the party now dominant in the Latin Church: the State must also be a slave.

Our Saviour had recognized as distinct the two provinces of the civil rule and the Church; had nowhere intimated that the spiritual authority was to claim the disposal of physical force, and to control in its own domain the authority which is alone responsible for external peace, order, and safety among civilized communities of men. It has been alike the peculiarity, the pride, and the misfortune of the Roman Church, among Christian communities, to allow to itself an unbounded use, as far as its power would go, of earthly instruments for spiritual ends. We have seen with what ample assurances this nation and Parliament were fed in 1826; how well and roundly the full and undivided rights of the civil power, and the separation of the two jurisdictions, were affirmed. All this had at length been undone, as far as Popes could undo it, in the Syllabus and the Encyclical. It remained to complete the undoing through the subserviency or pliability of the Council.

And the work is now truly complete. Lest it should be said that supremacy in faith and morals, full dominion over personal belief and conduct, did not cover the collective action of men in States, a third province was opened, not indeed to the abstract assertion of Infallibility, but to the far more practical and decisive demand of absolute Obedience. And this is the proper work of the Third Chapter, to which I am endeavoring to do a tardy justice. . . .

Absolute obedience, it is boldly declared, is due to the Pope, at the peril of salvation, not alone in faith, in morals, but in all things which concern the discipline and government of the Church. Thus are swept into the Papal net whole multitudes of facts, whole systems of government, prevailing, though in different degrees, in every country of the world. Even in the United States, where the severance between Church and State is supposed to be complete, a long catalogue might be drawn of subjects belonging to the domain and competency of the State, but also undeniably affecting the government of the Church; such as, by way of example, marriage, burial, education, prison discipline, blasphemy, poor-relief, incorporation, mortmain, religious endowments, vows of celibacy, and obedience. In Europe the circle is far wider, the points of contact and of interlacing almost innumerable. But on all matters respecting which any Pope may think proper to declare that they concern either faith or morals, or the government or discipline of the Church, he claims, with the approval of a Council undoubtedly Œcumenical in the Roman sense, the absolute obedience, at the peril of salvation, of every member of his communion.

It seems not as yet to have been thought wise to pledge the Council in terms to the Syllabus and the Encyclical. That achievement is probably reserved for some one of its sittings yet to come. In the meantime it is well to remember that this claim in respect of all things affecting the discipline and government of the Church, as well as faith and conduct, is lodged in open day by and in the reign of a Pontiff who has condemned free speech, free writing, a free press, toleration of nonconformity, liberty of conscience, the study of civil and philosophical matters in independence of the ecclesiastical authority, marriage unless sacramentally contracted, and the definition by the State of the civil rights (*jura*) of the Church; who has demanded for the Church, therefore, the title to define its own civil rights, together with a divine right to civil immunities, and a right to use physical force; and who has also proudly asserted that the Popes of the Middle Ages with their Councils did not invade the rights of princes: as for example, Gregory VII, of the Emperor Henry IV; Innocent III, of Raymond of Toulouse; Paul III, in deposing Henry VIII; or Pius V, in performing the like paternal office for Elizabeth.

I submit, then, that my fourth proposition [that she (Rome) has equally repudiated modern thought and ancient history] is true; and that England is entitled to ask, and to know, in what way the obedience required by the Pope and the Council of the Vatican is to be reconciled with the integrity of civil allegiance?

No Threat to Civil Allegiance

ARCHBISHOP MANNING

To the Editor of the Times. Archbishop's House, Westminster, 7th November 1874.

SIR — The gravity of the subject on which I address you, affecting, as it must, every Catholic in the British Empire, will, I hope, obtain from your courtesy the publication of this letter.

This morning I received a copy of a

The letter is reprinted in Edmund Sheridan Purcell, *Life of Cardinal Manning, Archbishop of Westminster* (New York: The Macmillan Company, 2 vols., 1895), vol. II, pp. 473–475. Reprinted with permission of the publisher.

pamphlet, entitled *The Vatican Decrees in their Bearing on Civil Allegiance*. I find in it a direct appeal to myself, both for the office I hold, and for the writings I have published. I gladly acknowledge the duty that lies upon me for both those reasons. I am bound by the office I bear not to suffer a day to pass without repelling from the Catholics of this country the lightest imputation upon their loyalty; and, for my teaching, I am ready to show that the principles I have ever taught are beyond impeachment upon that score.

It is true, indeed, that in page 57 of the pamphlet Mr. Gladstone expresses his belief "that many of his Roman Catholic friends and fellow-countrymen are, to say the least of it, as good citizens as himself." But as the whole pamphlet is an elaborate argument to prove that the teaching of the Vatican Council renders it impossible for them to be so, I cannot accept this grateful acknowledgment, which implies that they are good citizens because they are at variance with the Catholic Church.

I should be wanting in duty to the Catholics of this country and to myself if I did not give a prompt contradiction to this statement, and if I did not with equal promptness affirm that the loyalty of our civil allegiance is, not in spite of the teaching of the Catholic Church, but because of it.

The sum of the argument in the pamphlet just published to the world is this: — That by the Vatican decrees such a change has been made in the relations of Catholics to the Civil Power of States, that it is no longer possible for them to render the same undivided Civil allegiance as it was possible for Catholics to render before the promulgation of those Decrees.

In answer to this it is for the present sufficient to affirm —

1. That the Vatican Decrees have in no jot or tittle changed either the obligations or the conditions of Civil allegiance.

2. That the Civil allegiance of Catholics is as undivided as that of all Christians, and of all men who recognise a divine or natural moral law.

3. That the Civil allegiance of no man is unlimited; and therefore the Civil allegiance of all men who believe in God, or are governed by conscience, is in that sense divided.

4. In this sense, and in no other, can it be said with truth that the Civil allegiance of Catholics is divided. The Civil allegiance of every Christian man in England is limited by conscience and the Law of God; and the Civil allegiance of Catholics is limited neither less nor more.

The public peace of the British Empire has been consolidated in the last half century by the elimination of religious conflicts and inequalities from our laws. The empire of Germany might have been equally peaceful and stable if its statesmen had not been tempted in an evil hour to rake up the old fires of religious disunion. The hand of one man, more than any other, threw this torch of discord into the German Empire. The history of Germany will record the name of Dr. Ignatius von Döllinger as the author of this national evil. I lament, not only to read the name, but to trace the arguments of Dr. von Döllinger in the pamphlet before me. May God preserve these kingdoms from the public and private calamities which are visibly impending over Germany. The author of the pamphlet, in his first line, assures us that his "purpose is not polemic but pacific." I am sorry that so good an intention should have so widely erred in the selection of the means.

But my purpose is neither to criticise nor to controvert. My desire and my duty, as an Englishman, as a Catholic, and as a pastor, is to claim for my flock and for myself a Civil allegiance as pure, as true, and as loyal as is rendered by the distinguished author of the pamphlet, or by any subject of the British Empire. — Your obedient servant,   H. E. MANNING.

A Drastic Change in
the Relations of Church and State

COUNT BEUST

[*Conclusion of the Note of Foreign Minister Count Beust to the Austro-Hungarian Chargé d'Affaires Palomba-Caracciolo, presented to the Cardinal State Secretary on August 6, 1870*]

I authorize you to inform the Papal government that the ministerial council has decided to cancel the concordat. I believe that the decision is amply justified by existing circumstances. One cannot unconcernedly maintain relations with a power which presents itself as one without limits and without control. Admittedly, infallibility is to extend only to matters of faith and morals; it is, however, clear that he who cannot err also arrogates for himself the right to decide on what is important for faith and morals, and in this way alone decides on the limits of his competence.

The Papal encyclical of September 8, 1864 and the syllabus which is attached to it showed clearly enough, before the proclamation of infallibility, to what matters, in the view of the Holy See, infallibility is to be applied. Over against a power of this kind, the state, if it does not want to seize upon new means, must at least reestablish its complete freedom of action in order to be able to counter encroachments which are almost inevitable.

The Hungarian government, relying on an old privilege of the Apostolic King, is preparing to make use of the *Placetum regium* [which would forbid the publication of the Vatican decrees in Hungary]. As I have already mentioned, the formal abrogation of the concordat, the legal validity of which is contested in Hungary, need not be pronounced in a land in which it is not considered to be state law. This is, however, not the case in the Cisleithian lands [Austria], where it will be necessary to withdraw the imperial patent of November 5, 1855, which at that time gave legal validity to the concordat. This measure, which will be prepared without delay, seemed to us sufficient without resorting to the *Placetum regium* [royal permission for publication of church decrees] which would moreover be contrary to the liberal spirit of the Austrian fundamental laws, and would place bonds on that very freedom which these laws guarantee, especially for the conduct of Catholic worship.

The Imperial and Royal Government nevertheless is content to return to complete freedom of action in order to be armed against eventual interference by the power of the church, which was created by the decisions of the recent Council. This change, which has taken place in the person of one of the contracting powers, as well as the conditions which the other power insisted upon when the concordat was concluded, give the government the right, of which it now makes use, to consider this act as annulled. It has become impossible in practice to carry out most of the provisions of the concordat. For example, the rights and prerogatives of the Catholic church, which Article I seeks to guarantee, take on an entirely new meaning and an entirely different importance

From Alois Hudal, *Die Österreichische Vatikanbotschaft 1806–1918* (Munich: Pohl & Co., 1952), pp. 207–208. (Trans. Ernst and Louise Helmreich).

from the moment that Papal Infallibility is proclaimed. The teachings and discipline of the church, which is the subject of Article XXXIV move now into new areas. The oath of Austrian bishops, which according to the formula of Article XX swears faithfulness to the Emperor, now loses its real worth, if it is to have no other significance than the one recognized by the Pope.

I could cite many more examples to support my view that the concordat of August 18, 1855, actually and legally is annulled by the decrees of the recent Council. May the authorities in Rome take into account the situation as it now appears. We, on our part, are simply stating the actual situation which has been created without reference to our wishes. The Imperial and Royal Government has not arbitrarily taken the initiative to dissolve the concordat; it has rather only obeyed the necessity which the decisions of the church have forced upon it.

This is the point of view from which the Imperial and Royal Government has had to consider the situation and make its decisions. Would you inform the Papal government of this and transmit such explanations as will contribute to an understanding of the true meaning of our actions?

At the same time, assure the authorities that nothing is farther from our wishes than to give the signal for a new conflict between the church and secular power. If the latter re-establishes its liberty, it will assuredly not make use of it in any way inimical to the interests of religion. Inasmuch as the state defends its rights, it will continue to protect the rights and the freedom of the church. It demands nothing more than to live in peace with the church, which it respects and whose high mission it recognizes.

II. THE ROMAN QUESTION:
THE VATICAN AND UNITED ITALY

The Unification of Italy had taken place against the wishes of the Pope and deprived him of his temporal possessions, first the Romagna, the Marches and Umbria in 1860, and finally in 1870 Rome itself. Not only had the Papal States disappeared from the map, but bitter conflict had developed between the Pope and the political leaders of the Risorgimento. In 1850 Piedmont passed the famous Siccardi laws which abolished ecclesiastical courts, did away with the right of asylum attached to churches and holy places, cut down the number of holidays and their protection by civil law, and restricted the right of religious bodies to acquire property under deed or will without consent of the government. A law of 1855 dissolved many monasteries in Piedmont, and similar legislation had affected Umbria, the Marches, and Naples in 1860–1861. Yet there were still provinces in Italy where no dissolution had taken place. New laws in 1866 brought further dissolution of monastic orders throughout Italy, although some institutions were always exempted. About 1300 monastic establishments had been liquidated before the 1866 measures, and now some 25,000 followed. Disputes and many difficulties arose over the administration of funds from these confiscated lands, which were to be used to pension the dispossessed monastics and also provide educational and charitable endowments. There was also much controversy over the government approval of appointment to bishoprics. As was the practice in many countries, a law in Piedmont provided that no Papal act would be valid within the kingdom without the royal *exequatur* (consent) and similarly the *placet* was necessary for acts of diocesans. Moreover the *exequatur* was necessary before a bishop could take possession of his temporalities. The right of *exequatur* was specifically condemned in number 41 of the Syllabus of Errors. In the middle 1860's about one half the Italian sees were without a resident bishop. A civil marriage law had gone into effect on January 1, 1866, but it was openly flouted by many of the clergy. Similarly a law making seminarists liable to military service antagonized the church authorities.

The Law of Papal Guarantees

A. C. JEMOLO

With the establishment of Rome as the capital of Italy, the Italian government sought to establish a working basis with the Papacy by passing a Law of Papal Guarantees. This law is discussed in the following selection by A. C. Jemolo, a distinguished Italian historian and a specialist on church-state relations in Italy.

THE law of May 13th, 1871, known as the Law of Guarantees, was divided into two parts.

The first part related to the Holy See. Under its provisions the Pope was to be deprived of all his sovereign rights, retain-

A. C. Jemolo, *Church and State in Italy 1850–1950*, trans. David Moore (Oxford: Basil Blackwell, 1960), pp. 49–51. Reprinted by permission of Basil Blackwell.

ing possession only of the Vatican and Lateran Palaces and the villa of Castel Gandolfo. He was, however, to be accorded all the honours of a sovereign, including the rights of precedence conceded to him by Catholic rulers, and he could not be arraigned under Italian penal law even for acts not immediately connected with his ministry. This provision, which was in part opposed by the Left, constituted the crux of the whole matter. History afforded no precedent for the case of a citizen who could declare the State unlawful and even incite men to destroy it without being punished or restrained by the State, and who could make any accusation against foreign States with the knowledge that if they protested his own State would have to reply: 'We can do nothing.' Moreover, under the law those who attacked or wronged the Pope would be liable to the same penalties as were prescribed for similar offences against the King. The diplomatic corps accredited to the Holy See would be entitled to the same immunities and privileges as the diplomatic corps accredited to the King. The Pope would be allowed to maintain his traditional armed forces, consisting of Mobile Guards, Swiss Guards, Palatine Guards and gendarmes. All cardinals would be left free to take part in conclaves, even those who at the time were undergoing punishment for crimes against the State, and no ecclesiastic could be persecuted for having assisted in the drafting and dissemination of Papal bulls. In addition, the State agreed never to expel from Rome any ecclesiastic whose work lay in the city. The Pope was to be allowed to have his own telegraph office and to make use of the 'diplomatic bag'; and the State promised to make him an annual allowance of 3,225,000 lire. (It is a well-known fact that the Pope did not recognize the Law of Guarantees, protesting that it did not guarantee his independence — the tone of his protests changed with the passage of time. While the law remained in force he never emerged from the Vatican. He did not claim his allowance of 3,225,-000 lire, nor did he establish his own telegraph office.)

The second part of the law, concerning relations between Church and State, represented no more than a very timid attempt to put the principles of separatism into practice. The State renounced all control over the promulgation of new ecclesiastical laws and in general over acts of the ecclesiastical authorities. It ceased to require bishops to take an oath of allegiance, and it gave up the right to appoint them in regions where the King claimed that prerogative. It repudiated the King's claim (which the Pope regarded as invalid) to fill the office of Papal Legate in Sicily by right of inheritance. Meetings of Church Councils could in future be called without previous Government assent. But nominations to ecclesiastical benefices (not to non-beneficiary offices, however important) and transactions relating to the property of officially recognized ecclesiastical organizations remained subject to Government control.

As has already been stated, the Pope did not recognize the Law of Guarantees. All orthodox Catholics shared his view that it did not guarantee the independence of the Holy See and that the measure of freedom accorded did not compensate for the loss of the temporal power. And yet, among these Catholics, it became more and more necessary to distinguish between the few who continued even after 1870 to hope for a return to the *status quo* of the years prior to 1859, and the remainder who, while they regarded the present situation as bad or even calamitous, cherished no such illusions as this. Already the Italian State had weathered one major storm in the shape of the guerrilla war, conducted in part by Bourbon sympathizers and in part by armed brigands, which had raged for years over a large part of the former Kingdom of Naples. It had survived the military defeat of 1866 and the disappearance from the scene of its great protector, Napoleon III. There was as yet no sign of the emergence of a Catholic monarch who would be willing to unsheathe the sword for the purpose of restoring the temporal power to the Papacy. Accordingly, men began to consider the possibility of bringing about a Catholic revival by lawful means, of winning over the Kingdom of Italy, now an inescapable reality, to the Catholic faith and of reforming its legislation. So far as the Law of Guarantees in particular was concerned, it was not long before those who moved even in Vatican circles, while insisting on its inadequacy, began to weigh its advantages. As a result, there was consternation whenever it seemed likely that the reins of government would fall into the hands of elements which might be expected to consider the law anew.

The Continuing Feud

S. WILLIAM HALPERIN

The Pope, having refused to accept the settlement proffered by the Italian State, withdrew to his compartments and became the "Prisoner of the Vatican." The unsolved problems of the years of the Risorgimento remained. In the selection below, Professor S. William Halperin of the University of Chicago discusses this continuing church-state feud and its repercussions in other countries. In addition to the volume from which this account is abridged, he has written a study on *Separation of Church and State in Italian Thought* and other distinguished volumes on Modern European History.

THE implacable hostility of the Vatican to the new order of things in the peninsula spurred the Italian government to take drastic measures against the church and its recalcitrant hierarchy. Decisive, too, in the launching of this concerted offensive was the eagerness of the country's rulers to accelerate the secularization of Italian life. The treatment accorded newly appointed bishops bespoke the mood of Lanza and his colleagues. The retention of the *exequatur* for the assignment of temporalities placed in the hands of the cabinet a powerful weapon of coercion of which it now proceeded to make ample use. It filled the ultramontane camp with consternation by announcing that it would grant the *exequatur* only to those recipients of the miter who presented their bulls of appointment to the political authorities. The Vatican replied that, with the scrapping of the old concordats and the separation of church and state in Italy, ecclesiastical appointees were under no obligation to proffer such deference to the civil power. This was the formal ground. More conclusive was the necessity of shunning any gesture, however innocuous, which might be construed as a recognition of the existing political order. Obeying the injunctions of the pope, new incumbents of episcopal sees late in 1871 refused to apply for the *exequatur*. The government promptly retaliated by denying them possession of their benefices. As a result, many bishops were constrained to take up quarters outside

From S. William Halperin, *Italy and the Vatican at War. A Study of Their Relations from the Outbreak of the Franco-Prussian War to the Death of Pius IX* (Chicago: The University of Chicago Press, 1939, Copyright 1939, The University of Chicago), pp. 282–471 *passim*. Abridged and reprinted by permission of the author and the publisher.

their official residences and depend upon subsidies from the Holy See. . . .

No less drastic were the measures directed against the intrenched position of the church in the field of education. The first blows were struck in Rome. When the Italians occupied the city, they found the clergy in charge of all elementary instruction. The Jesuits established in the Collegio romano were the sole dispensers of secondary education, while the University of Rome had been ruthlessly purged of instructors suspected of liberal sympathies. The cabinet, aided by the Giunta, at once took up the question of secularizing the city's educational system. The new public schools were housed in the Collegio romano, with only a portion of that edifice reserved for the use of the Jesuits. The latter reopened their schools early in November, but the outcry which greeted this gesture led to the imposition of a ban on teaching by members of the hated order. Visconti-Venosta, in a circular dated November 25, 1870, defended the closing of the Jesuit schools and invoked the law of the kingdom to justify the establishment, in their stead, of state-controlled institutions of secondary education.

Article XIII of the law of guarantees provided that Catholic seminaries in Rome and in the suburbicarian sees were to continue under the aegis of the Holy See, without any state interference at all. However, the government was declared qualified to intervene whenever anything should be taught in them which was contrary to the laws of the land. Difficulties speedily arose when these seminaries proceeded to admit large numbers of lay as well as clerical students. Moderates and radicals were at one in assailing this action. According to one eminent authority on constitutional law, Article XIII had reference only to the training of candidates for the priesthood. Were the seminaries to impart instruction to any and all students, they would forfeit their special immunity and become subject, like all other educational institutions, to the supervision of the state.

Acting on this interpretation of the article, the government dispatched inspectors to some of the seminaries. The latter, however, bolted their doors to these representatives of the civil power. The cabinet accepted the challenge. In August, 1872, it ordered the closing of the recalcitrant institutions. This produced results. The ecclesiastical authorities relented, and the ministerial order was revoked. The following December the ministry of public instruction issued a circular which formally resolved the issue of the controversy. It laid down the principle that the ecclesiastical hierarchy was free to determine the curriculum of candidates for the priesthood. It added, however, that, whenever seminaries should be opened to lay and foreign students, the regulations of the civil educational authorities would have to be complied with. . . .

Much more significant was the problem of religious instruction in public institutions. The secularism which inspired the government's attitude in this matter was clearly attested by the introduction of a bill abolishing the chairs of theology in all the state universities. The enactment of such a measure had long been one of the objectives of Italian liberalism. . . .

The bill was discussed in the chamber late in April, 1872. Its opponents, led by Gonghi, made a valiant effort to defeat it. They warned that its effect would be to give the church a monopoly in the teaching of theology. This, they contended, was but one of the dire consequences that might be expected to ensue. Others were the destruction of the unity of the church and the decline of Catholic sentiment. On the other hand, retention of the chairs in question would rebound to the advantage of both Italy and the church. Specifically, it would improve the prospects of a religious peace in the peninsula. The ministerial defenders of the measure, headed by Correnti, argued that church and state were distinct entities with well-articulated objectives of their own and that progress could be achieved only by allowing each to go its own way without interference from the other. Furthermore, the state, in accordance with the separatist principle proclaimed in the law of guarantees, was not qualified to have any hand in the teaching of theology. This proved to be one of the rare occasions on which the Sinistra [party of the left] saw eye to eye with the government, and a somewhat heterogeneous majority was mustered to pass the bill. The outcry in the clerical press was loud and sustained. . . .

Correnti's concurrent attempt to eliminate religious instruction from the secondary schools of the country proved less successful, however. The almost unanimous opposition which this bill encountered among moderates both in and out of parliament led in May to its withdrawal by the cabinet and the resignation of the minister of public instruction.

The change recently instituted in the status of religious instruction in the elementary schools was particularly galling to the clericals. The famous Casati law of 1859 had made the teaching of religion obligatory in all the primary educational institutions of the state. Non-Catholics, however, were free to secure exemption for their children by declaring that they would furnish such instruction privately. This arrangement had been the target of persistent criticism during the ensuing years. It had been argued that it was a flagrant violation of the freedom of conscience and utterly incompatible with the separation of church and state. Not infrequently, prefects and local school boards had advised the government that the teaching of religion was properly the function of the family and not of the state. These counsels finally prevailed. Circulars issued on September 29, 1870, and July 12, 1871, by the ministry of public instruction reversed the situation created by the Casati law. Religious instruction was hereafter to be imparted only to those children whose parents explicitly requested it. The teaching of religion in the elementary schools was thus relegated to a very subordinate place in the curricular hierarchy. . . .

No less severe was the government's treatment of monastic orders. Laws enacted in 1866 and 1867 and inspired in no small degree by financial considerations had proclaimed the suppression of all religious corporations in Italy. No sooner had the remnants of the papal state conquered in 1870 been incorporated into the Italian kingdom than a great hue and cry went up from anticlericals of every description in favor of the immediate extension of these laws to this most recent territorial acquisition. Once again, economic factors reinforced the doctrinaire zeal of these opponents of the church, for more than one-third of the land in the city and province of Rome was held in mortmain. In March, 1871, a proposal sponsored by Mancini brought the issue before the chamber of deputies. The government, in its anxiety to spare as far as possible the susceptibilities of the Vatican, was resolved to proceed slowly in this delicate matter. . . .

On June 16, 1872, in a strongly worded letter to Antonelli, Pius himself directed a vigorous broadside against the contemplated abolition of these pillars of the church. He recapitulated all the woes beginning with the events of September 20, 1870. The outrage now to be perpetrated, he charged, was simply part of an infernal scheme to undermine his position as head of the church. He alluded to the continual encroachments upon his jurisdiction and declared that he could never enjoy freedom and independence as long as he was subject to "the tyranny and caprice of a hostile authority." Everything that was happening in Rome, he asserted, was convincing proof that the law of guarantees was a ghastly joke. "Of what use is it," he queried, "to proclaim the immunity of the pope's person and residence, when the government is not strong enough to safeguard us from the daily insults to which our authority is exposed . . . ? Of what use is it to proclaim the liberty of our pastoral ministry when all the legislation . . . is in open conflict with the fundamental principles and universal laws of the church?" Antonelli was instructed to acquaint the diplomatic corps at the Vatican with the true state of affairs. . . . "Foreign governments," Pius wrote, "cannot forget that the pontifical throne, far from being a hindrance to the peace and prosperity of Europe, or to the greatness and independence of Italy, was always a bond between peoples and princes, and always a source of concord and peace. It was for Italy a source of real greatness, a guardian of her independence, and the constant defense and rampart of her liberty." If every Catholic had the right to ask his government to protect his own religious freedom, he was equally entitled to demand that it guarantee the liberty of the head of his church. It was incumbent upon all governments "to defend and protect the most legitimate cause on earth, certain, as they should be, that, in supporting the sacred rights of the Roman pontiff, they are defending and protecting their own."

This passionate appeal made no little impression in foreign capitals, but the governments could scarcely do more than offer platonic expressions of commiseration. . . . The [Italian] cabinet's first impulse, on perusing the pope's missive, was to draft a considerably harsher bill than the one which it had originally planned. But in the end it relented, partly out of deference to the friendly representations of Austria and France. The second article of the bill which it submitted to parliament on November 20 made an exception in favor of the generals of the doomed orders. It permitted them to remain in the edifices which had hitherto served as their headquarters in Rome. . . .

The fate of the generals was the paramount issue of prolonged and acrimonious parliamentary debates in the spring of 1873. The chamber reporting committee proposed the retention of the generalship houses. They were indispensable, it held, to the Holy See in the discharge of its spiritual functions. But it recommended

that only a portion of these buildings be allotted to the heads of the orders for the duration of their period of office. The government somewhat reluctantly acquiesced in this modification. But the leftists refused to countenance any arrangement which would keep the generals and their staffs in Rome. . . .

Minghetti, who was destined very shortly to replace Lanza as premier, ably defended the ministerial view. There was universal agreement, he pointed out, that the religious orders should be abolished as juridical entities and that mortmain should be completely done away with. But it was also important to see that a rigid application of the laws of 1866–67 to Rome would be unwise. The exceptional circumstances in the former papal capital, together with the exigencies of the new church-state system inaugurated with the law of guarantees, called for a less drastic procedure. It was the necessity of giving the pontiff the most ample freedom in his relations with foreign Catholics that constrained the government to deal more leniently with the generals of the orders. Visconti-Venosta spoke in like fashion. He explained that the cabinet, in order to be faithful to the spirit of the law of guarantees, had to ascertain whether any of the religious institutions now in Rome were essential to the government of the universal church. It was clear, he continued, that the generalships belonged in this category. They were, without a doubt, indispensable instruments of the pope's spiritual ministry and inseparable from his relations with the Catholic world. Only the timely intervention of Baron Ricasoli averted a deadlock. With distracted deputies looking about for a Moses to lead them out of the parliamentary wilderness, he suggested a compromise which proved acceptable to the chamber. He proposed that the recommendations of the committee be made optional rather than mandatory in their effect. The government was to be authorized to permit the generals to occupy their present quarters until their terms of office should expire. But it was to be clearly understood that the minister in charge of this matter was to be entirely free in deciding whether or not to make use of this authority. . . .

With the thorniest issue disposed of, the bill moved swiftly forward to enactment. It received the approval of the chamber on May 27 and that of the senate on June 17. In thus divesting the religious corporations of their juridical personality, the Italian legislators believed that they were carrying into effect one of the logical consequences of the separation of church and state. Actually, the most significant feature of the law was the destruction of the last vestiges of mortmain in the peninsula. The Vatican had been worsted, but its loyal defenders came away from the struggle echoing the *Osservatore romano's* parting dictum that the law was "a horrible injustice and a violation of all rights."

The attempts of the state to destroy the church's ancient monopoly in the field of marriage proved another fecund source of friction. Civil matrimony had been incorporated into the code issued in 1865 and put into effect on January 1, 1866. Openly flouting the terms of this statute, numerous devout couples contented themselves with the celebration of the religious rites and refused to appear before the civil magistrates. It was in vain that the *Opinione* exhorted the clergy to refrain from performing the religious ceremony if the civil formalities had not previously been complied with. Defiance of the marriage law, instead of abating, assumed ever increasing proportions. Yielding to the clamor of anticlericals in the chamber and in the country at large, the government, in October, 1872, ordered the royal procurators to make a thorough investigation of the situation. The data thus gathered convinced the cabinet that drastic intervention was required. In December of the following year it submitted to parliament a bill stipulating that the civil had always to precede the religious ceremony. Severe penalties for the infraction of this regulation were prescribed. Vigliani, the minister of justice,

made it very plain to the chamber just why the government was taking an action which was clearly at variance with the separatist principle embodied in the law of guarantees. He pointed out that during the period from January 1, 1866, to December 31, 1871, no fewer than 120,421 marriages had been solemnized with the church sacrament alone. The Sinistra loudly supported the ministry. . . .

The bill, however, speedily encountered formidable opposition. The clericals were furious, and loud protest was registered by the Italian episcopate. The *Osservatore romano* insisted that the clergy had faithfully endeavored to persuade all Catholics to comply with the law on civil matrimony. If that law was being ignored, it was not the fault of the priests. "The Italian people," the papal sheet went on to explain, "is profoundly Catholic. Believing that matrimony is a sacrament, it finds it difficult to understand what the magistrate has to do with it, and therefore to appear before him seems almost a sacrilege. . . ." The clerical daily [*Voce della verità*] reminded its adversaries that the sacrament of marriage was regarded as holy by all peoples that had attained any degree of civilization. But the teachings of men like Maillet and Lamarck, it jeered, had changed all this. They had discovered that men originated from fish or Cete. And now it was being demonstrated that gorillas or macaques were the progenitors of the human species. In accordance with these notions, it was believed that matrimony too was something "bestial" and that the most sacred of unions could be consummated by a contract in exactly the same way that a horse was purchased or a house rented. The idea of having a contract solemnized in the presence of the mayor was "an egregious discovery of that dear French Revolution to which we owe immortal benefits," and the Italian government, with characteristic perversity, had imitated the French. . . .

The Catholic party was not alone in demanding the defeat of the bill. Large sections of moderate opinion, too, were outraged. They held that the proposed law was inconsistent with the country's established policy of affording the maximum liberty to all citizens and in conflict with the principle of the freedom of the church. Moreover, they were inclined to believe that infractions of the civil marriage law were due to ignorance and negligence rather than to ill will. . . . The quality of the opposition induced the government to reconsider the question, and the bill was allowed to lapse. Nor was the issue immediately revived with the advent of the Sinistra in 1876. The latter sought to explain its failure to deal promptly with this ticklish matter by alleging a reduction in the number of marriages contracted without the civil formalities. It was not until 1879 that the entire problem was again discussed in the Italian parliament.

TESTING THE LAW OF GUARANTEES

During the initial months of 1874, rumors of an inpending peace between Quirinal and Vatican caused something of a stir throughout the peninsula. Unquestionably, many devout Catholics would have welcomed an Italo-papal understanding. They were aware that a final settlement of the issues involved would necessarily require much time, but they hoped that at least some preliminary steps in the right direction might be taken without undue delay. . . .

Many Italian clericals, inspired by a sense of their growing strength, believed that the moment had come to discard the *nè eletti nè elettori* [neither elected, nor electors] formula. Parliamentary elections, the first since the transfer of the capital to Rome, were scheduled for November, and during the preceding months not a few influential Catholics pronounced themselves in favor of mass participation. They contended that abstention, though it represented a logically consistent course, only worked injury to the real interests of the church. On the other hand, much good might come from recourse to the polls. It

would be possible, once a considerable number of chamber seats had been captured, to frustrate the machinations of the anticlericals. But the Vatican was adamant in its refusal to countenance such a *volte-face*. It was frankly skeptical of its ability to secure by parliamentary methods, any appreciable improvement of its position. . . . On October 13 he [Pius IX] silenced the dissidents within the flock by publicly reaffirming the *non expedit*. He could not, he said, permit Catholics to accept seats in the chamber of deputies. For one thing, the elections were not free, owing to the interplay of political passions. And, even if this were not so, there was the insuperable obstacle of the oath required of all deputies — an oath which signified acquiescence in the existing political order. Therefore, he concluded, Catholics would have to continue to stay away from the chamber. The *Civiltà cattolica*, commenting authoritatively on the meaning of the papal pronouncement, declared that the ban imposed upon the acceptance of seats in the chamber was equally applicable to voting in parliamentary elections. And the *Osservatore romano*, alluding to the government's plea for support against the ever growing leftist threat, followed the *Unità cattolica* in pronouncing the Destra [moderate rightist party] as bad as the Sinistra. "They are all sectarians," it charged, "all enemies of the pope, all oppressors of religion."

The Italian government was keenly disappointed, as it had hoped to the last for electoral support from Catholic conservatives. But despite the defection of these potential allies, it was determined to persist in the moderate ecclesiastical policy inaugurated after the fall of the Lanza cabinet. Of this determination it was now to give striking proof. On February 5, 1875, Pius issued an encyclical which declared the May laws null and void and released Prussian Catholics from obedience to them. At once there was a great outcry in Germany. The ministerial and liberal press declaimed in the strongest language against the pontiff and deplored the impunity with which this bold gesture had been made. One writer close to Bismarck pronounced the encyclical a declaration of war which dissolved all previous compacts between Prussia and the Roman see. . . . Throughout 1874 the alleged meekness of the Italian government vis-à-vis the Vatican in such matters as the recognition of episcopal appointments, the assignment of temporalities, and the execution of the civil marriage law had drawn much acrid comment from the German press, and these complaints had been pronounced justified by leftist circles in the peninsula. . . .

Bismarck's criticism of Italian ecclesiastical policy spurred the Sinistra to force a showdown on the church-state issue. For several months, charges of inexcusable submissiveness and laxity vis-à-vis the Holy See had been directed at the government. Official acquiescence in attempts by the church to overstep the bounds of its authority had been alleged. Not a few moderates had joined their leftist compatriots in denouncing the excessively indulgent attitude of the political authorities toward clerical defiance of existing ecclesiastical legislation. . . . There were two important counts in this indictment. One was the alleged failure of the authorities to withhold the temporalities from those bishops who had refused to comply with the *exequatur* clause of the law of guarantees. The other was the do-nothing attitude of the government in the face of papal efforts to foment revolution in Germany. The cabinet's critics insisted further that the clergy was being permitted to plot with impunity against the national interests. . . .

During the next few months the government commenced a wholesale expulsion from their sees of those prelates who had refused to comply with the *exequatur* clause. The Vatican indignantly countered with the charge that this "persecution" was being carried out at the behest of Berlin. The lull in the Italo-papal feud which had followed the accession of Minghetti was clearly at an end. . . .

In March, 1876, Destra rule finally came to an end when the Minghetti government went down to defeat on a motion relating to the unpopular *macinato* or flour tax. A parliamentary revolution of the first magnitude occurred with the advent of a Sinistra cabinet headed by Agostino Depretis, the veteran politician who had succeeded Rattazzi as the leader of the opposition. The antecedents of the country's new rulers were well calculated to fill the Vatican with profound foreboding. Depretis himself was a Freemason and a staunch liberal. His program, as he had stated it the previous autumn, comprised the extension of secular education, the defense of the state's traditional prerogatives, the prosecution of clerical calumniators, and the lay administration of ecclesiastical properties. The *Diritto*, which speedily came to be regarded as the new premier's special mouthpiece, minced no words in proclaiming that the era of half-way measures was past. "Germany," it predicted, "will find Italy . . . aiding her vigorously to carry on the course she has adopted." The Depretis cabinet, according to the Sinistra journal, was determined to safeguard the civil authority against clerical abuses. It was likewise interested in certain sweeping reforms. It wished to secularize the administration of ecclesiastical properties, emancipate the lower clergy, and develop public instruction. But it was resolved, at the same time, to preserve the law of guarantees. And it had no thought of impeding in any way the convocation of the next papal conclave.

The program foreshadowed in this newspaper pronouncement boded ill for the future of church-state relations. And indeed, with the accession of the Sinistra, Italian ecclesiastical policy became definitely more severe. Late in March, Depretis himself intimated in the chamber of deputies that darker times were ahead for the church. His government, he said, would be neither aggressive nor hostile in its ecclesiastical policy. But it likewise had no intention of being conciliatory. The existing laws would be firmly enforced, even though they were dictated by "a political prudence which experience has shown to be excessive but which in any case should not be repudiated without grave and new reasons." That was not all, however. He and his ministerial colleagues felt obliged to take legislative action to protect "freedom of conscience and the rights of society" against abuses, committed in the exercise of the spiritual office. This declaration of policy left the clericals with few illusions. . . .

The new cabinet wasted no time in demonstrating its mettle. Late in March, Pius felicitated Bishop Dupanloup for having protested against the recently enacted law abolishing the exemption of Italian clerics from military service. The papal letter contained some very unflattering allusions to the Italian government, and a ministerial decree was issued forbidding its publication in Rome. The *Osservatore romano* disregarded the ban and reproduced the document in its issue of April 23, 1876. It was promptly confiscated by the authorities, much to the indignation of the clericals, who signalized the incident as still another proof of the futility of the law of guarantees. Bismarck, they wailed, was exerting pressure upon his Sinistra friends in an effort to get them to wage war against the Catholic church. . . . This outcry, however, made little impression upon Depretis and his associates. They had only begun the long-deferred task of subjugating the ecclesiastical hierarchy. Late in July, Nicotera [Minister of Interior] forbade outdoor religious processions, alleging that they were deleterious to the maintenance of public order. This measure, according to the Sinistra apologists, was entirely defensible. The government possessed the right to prohibit religious processions in the interests of public health, safety, and tranquillity. In any case — so ran the argument — religious processions were unnecessary. They were reminiscent of pagan celebrations and had been discontinued in many civilized countries. . . .

The clericals once again complained of religious persecution. . . . Pius himself protested against the ban in an address before a group of Savoyard pilgrims.

This clamor, too, went unheeded. The offensive against the church was pushed with unabated ardor. In September the minister of the interior ordered drastic action to halt the stealthy resurrection of religious orders. . . . Satisfied that the drift of public opinion was favorable to his party's chances, Depretis announced new chamber elections for November 5. Throughout the ensuing campaign, he kept the ecclesiastical question in the foreground as one of the issues on which the nation and the Sinistra were in entire accord. The law of guarantees, he told his constituency early in October, represented "a transition or a transaction . . . between the past and the future" — a dictum with which few of his countrymen could disagree. Religion, he triumphantly continued, had been whittled down to its proper stature — that of an abstract bond. . . .

The oratorical broadsides of the premier and of his lieutenants, coupled with skilful electioneering, contributed significantly to the triumph of the ministerialists. The popular tendency to associate the rule of the moderates with onerous tax burdens did the rest. The bulk of the nation, which had had its fill of Destra finance, was of no mind to oust its new rulers, and the Depretis government emerged with a decisive victory at the polls. The offensive against the church could now be resumed with far better prospect of complete success. . . .

On November 20, Victor Emmanuel informed the new parliament that Italy was about to embark upon a Kulturkampf of her own. "It remains for us," he said, "to face a problem hitherto not dealt with. The freedom conceded the church in our kingdom far exceeds that enjoyed by it in any other Catholic state. But it cannot be so exercised as to violate public liberty or infringe upon the national sovereignty." The import of the royal announcement was all too clear to the Vatican. The *Osservatore romano* warned its readers that they could now expect "an aggravation of the war against the church, more sectarian greed to be appeased at public expense, further larcenies, and more extended propaganda in favor of public corruption." On November 25 the so-called clerical abuses bill made its appearance in the chamber of deputies. It imposed severe penalties upon priests guilty of abusing their spiritual functions to disturb the "public conscience" and the "peace of families," censure the laws and institutions of the state, and encourage resistance to the acts of the public authorities.

The chamber debate opened on January 18, 1877. The anticlericals who now dominated the lower house seized the opportunity to attack the pope, the church, and the Catholic faith in language of unprecedented violence. Petruccelli led the onslaught. "The church," he asserted, "has always been subversive. After the Vatican council, it became aggressive. After September 20, it became hydrophobic." He could write a volume, he said, were he to record all the "antisocial, immoral, perverse doctrines of the church, the Holy Father, and the Vatican." He would vote for the bill, even though it was not sufficiently drastic. For it did, after all, consecrate "the principle of the sovereignty of the state." The debate was enlivened by the valiant attempt of the conservative deputy, Bortolucci, to restrain his radical colleagues. He deplored the irreverent tone of the preceding speakers who had spared neither the church nor its venerable head. . . .

THE BATTLE OVER THE CLERICAL ABUSES BILL

The chamber vote of January 24, 1877 [which passed the bill], was a challenge, and the Vatican was not loath to accept it. . . . Throughout the peninsula the defenders of the church rallied to ward off the impending blow. Protest after protest against the clerical abuses bill appeared in all the ultramontane newspapers. One of the most telling broadsides came from the spokesmen of the Roman Society for Catholic Interests. The burden of their indictment was that one class, the clergy, was being penalized and persecuted, that an attempt was being made to silence the pope as well as his subordinates, and that revolt against the legitimate ecclesiastical authorities was being shamelessly fomented. Pius himself, in a stirring allocution delivered on March 12, lashed out furiously against the ecclesiastical policy of the Quirinal and appealed to Catholics throughout the world to induce their governments to intervene on his behalf. This consistorial pronouncement — easily the most violent of the many utterances which had emanated from the Vatican since the occupation of Rome — was in a sense the aged pontiff's political testament. Never before had he so unequivocally asserted that the existence of a united Italy was incompatible with independence of the Holy See. It was his purpose to proclaim a sort of crusade against Italy. The Catholic powers, with France, so he hoped, in their van, were to be prevailed upon to throw themselves into this holiest of enterprises. Copies of the papal address were sent to the members of the diplomatic corps accredited to the Vatican. They were also the recipients of a note from Cardinal Simeoni expressing the hope that they would convey to their governments the facts cited by the Holy Father. . . .

It was the attitude not of the governments but of their Catholic subjects that cheered the Vatican. The allocution of March 12 had stirred the masses of the faithful everywhere, and impressive indeed were the manifestations of loyalty which poured in upon the Holy Father in response to his request for aid. Spanish Catholics proclaimed their solidarity with the pontiff and adjured their government to recall its minister from the Quirinal. On April 2 the Catholic Union of Great Britain plunged into the fray with a formidable protest against the clerical abuses bill. The Belgian episcopate, headed by

Cardinal Deschamps, the Archbishop of Malines, implored King Leopold II to bestir himself in the pope's behalf. German clericals vented their indignation in a fiery manifesto which denounced the Mancini circular as "a direct attack against the rights of the church" and as "a monstrous and infamous assault upon the Catholics of all nations." On May 1 the first general assembly of Austrian Catholics unanimously pledged itself to work for "the termination of the pope's sufferings." After a discussion in which less intrepid spirits were given a perfunctory hearing, it decided to send an address to the emperor invoking his aid. These gestures, in themselves of no extraordinary account, assumed special significance in the light of the current Austro-Italian tension over Balkan affairs.

Nowhere was the agitation more intense and more anti-Italian in character than in France. . . . The battle began in earnest when the general assembly of French Catholics early in April issued a call for a nation-wide campaign. In a petition addressed to the president, the senate, and the chamber of deputies, it insisted that the pope, bereft of his territorial sovereignty, was finding it increasingly difficult to discharge his spiritual functions. There was a real danger, it warned, that he might soon be prevented from communicating with his flock throughout the world. "In view of so serious a situation," it continued, "French citizens and Catholics . . . feel it their duty to appeal to you. They ask you to employ all the means which are in your power to make the Holy Father's independence respected, to protect his administration, and to insure to the Catholics of France the indispensable enjoyment of a liberty dearer than all others — that of their conscience and faith. . . .

All eyes were focused on the Italian senate, in whose hands lay the fate of the much-discussed bill. The clamor of foreign Catholics had not facilitated the task of the opposition. Senators of moderate sympathies who from the first had doubted the wisdom of exceptional laws against any section of the population were repelled by the spectacle of alien bishops and priests inciting their governments to intervene in the affairs of Italy. The *Opinione* played upon the sensibilities of these vacillating members of the upper house. It was true, it repeated, that the government had acted rather tactlessly. But in view of the battle being launched by clerical reactionaries throughout Europe, it would be reprehensible to give them a victory in this particular test. In a state of war all citizens had to do their duty, even if their government were guilty of committing an error. But, despite the efforts of Sella and the split within the ranks of the Destra, the measure was defeated on May 7 by a majority which persisted in regarding it as both untimely and tyrannical. According to one reliable source, word of this unexpected denouement evoked from the pontiff a laconic "Thank God! . . ."

THE END OF A PONTIFICATE

Less publicized than the clerical abuses bill, but an even more telling gesture against the power of the church in Italy, was the measure announced by Coppino in the spring of 1876. It called for the establishment of compulsory instruction for all children who had attained the age of six. It thus placed the state in direct competition with the ecclesiastical hierarchy as the dispenser of primary education. The outcry in the clerical press was loud and sustained. "Italian liberty," prophesied the *Osservatore romano*, "will receive a new and lethal blow through the law on obligatory instruction, which is destined . . . to violate the most sacrosanct of rights, that exercised by parents over the education of their children." But that was not all, in the opinion of the papal organ. State-controlled education would mean the prevalence in Italy of the most abysmal ignorance. Even more violent was the language of the *Unità cattolica*. The proposed measure, it raged, was "such an enormity that we can scarcely find words strong enough to designate it properly." It was part of a scheme "to corrupt the minds and hearts" of Italian children. For obligatory instruction was nothing less than the offspring of modern socialism.

The chamber debate occurred early in March, 1877. The extremist fringe of the Sinistra majority was not altogether satisfied with the terms of the bill. Led by Petruccelli and Bovio, it urged the total exclusion of religious instruction from the schools of the state. The *Diritto* heartily indorsed this position. It demanded that only secular instruction be imparted in the nation's schools, alleging that the clergy was intent upon exploiting its teaching functions to recruit supporters for the ultramontane party. But the cabinet, though its sympathies were with these militants, appreciated the difficulty of completely laicizing public education and persuaded the chamber to reject that proposal. It accepted with alacrity the alternative one offered by Benedetto Cairoli, another notorious anticlerical. He suggested that religious instruction be made purely optional and that it be given only at the request of the parents and at special hours. Thus, the law, which was finally promulgated on July 15, reaffirmed the principle already laid down in the circulars of 1870 and 1871. Throughout the parliamentary discussion of the bill the moderate press gave the ministry its unstinted support. It hailed the chamber's approval of the measure as a victory for a government "which proposes something just and wise" and urged prompt senatorial indorsement. The Vatican's organs, continuing their spirited campaign against Coppino's project, decried the attempt to secularize all elementary instruction as an assault against freedom. Modern liberalism, one of them charged, "rejects liberty in fact because it feels it cannot live. . . . by liberty, because it itself is really the worst of tyrannies." The idea of obligatory education was again vehemently arraigned, and the political authorities were warned that "honest"

heads of families preferred religious instruction for their children. . . .

It was in the midst of these lively polemics that Victor Emmanuel was fatally stricken. He died on January 9, after he had received the last sacraments of the Church from his chaplain, Mgr. Anzino. "I die like a Catholic," the monarch was reported to have said during these closing lugubrious moments. "I have never done anything with the idea of offending the church. I regret that the decisions I have had to make in the interests of Italy should have been the cause of sorrow to the pope." He was reputed to have added that, in everything he had done, he had been certain in his own mind that he was fulfilling his duties as a citizen and as a ruler. His death came as a great shock, and intense indeed was the grief of the nation. The pontiff himself partook of the general mourning. On first learning of the king's illness he had asked to be kept minutely informed as to his condition. . . . On the morning of the ninth, when the bulletins from the Quirinal indicated that the end was near, Pius said to one of his attendants that the passing of Victor Emmanuel would be a misfortune for everyone, including the Vatican. When informed that his royal adversary was no more, he was reported to have exclaimed: "He died like a Christian, like a sovereign, and like an honorable man!" The charity displayed by His Holiness on this occasion was emulated by the more responsible ultramontane journals. The *Voce della verità* spoke highly of the deceased ruler's ability and acknowledged his moderation. He combined, in its opinion, "courageous intelligence, prudent courage, and strength of purpose in any path with a clearly traced and firmly pursued aim. . . ." But not all the clerical sheets showed such generosity. So abusive was the language of some of them in commenting upon the death of the king that even certain members of the sacred college protested to the pope. . . .

Rome was decided upon as the site of interment, in the face of bitter opposition from the citizens of Turin. The latter insisted that the king's remains should be preserved in the mausoleum of the Superga, just outside the Piedmontese capital, which housed the tombs of all of Victor Emmanuel's Savoyard ancestors. But grave political considerations, apart from the attitude of the Romans themselves, impelled the government to ignore the claims of the Turinese. One contemporary observer justly appreciated the situation when he wrote:

It was feared that taking the body of Victor Emmanuel from Rome might give rise to the idea at the Vatican that the House of Savoy did not consider itself sufficiently secure of its permanent tenure of Rome. The good sense of the Italian people comprehended the evil which might accrue had the clerical party a pretext of affirming that the House of Savoy carried away their dead from the field of battle like an acknowledgment of their defeat.

. . . Feeble and ailing as he was, the indefatigable pontiff girded himself for a devastating pronouncement on the subject of Humbert's accession. But he did not live to make it. He died on February 7, leaving to his successor the grim business of continuing the feud which he had waged so relentlessly. Thus ended a pontificate which one writer has called "the most tempestuous in the entire history of the church." On this occasion, the press and public opinion, irrespective of party, gave an exemplary demonstration of tact and fair-mindedness. Journals of every description paid the deceased warm tribute.

Catholics in National Politics

RICHARD A. WEBSTER

In 1868 Pius IX (1846–1878) issued a decree *non expedit* which stated that it was not expedient for Catholics to vote in parliamentary elections. This was a paramount factor in accounting for the failure to organize in Italy a Catholic-dominated political party such as the Center party in Germany. *Non expedit* was repeatedly confirmed and strengthened in the next decades. In spite of these Papal pronouncements many Italians voted in parliamentary elections, but at the same time adhered to the church and considered themselves Catholics. Eventually with the growth of socialist parties this policy was relaxed, as is indicated in this selection by Professor Richard A. Webster of the University of California, Berkeley.

IN the 1870's and 1880's the intransigent Catholic press battled unceasingly against the State and the Liberal ruling class. Italy's economic and social troubles furnished excellent issues: the increasing tax burdens and cost of living, rising unemployment, speculation in Church properties seized by the State and sold to the *bourgeoisie*, were all laid to the account of Italian Liberalism, guilty not only of heresy but also of social exploitation. Intransigent Catholic agitation took on a democratic and even demagogic tone with the passage of time.

The intransigents, with their everlasting jeremiads against the new Italy, by no means represented the Italian Catholic laity as such. Many Catholics had worked

Reprinted from *The Cross and the Fasces* pp. 5–8 by Richard A. Webster with the permission of the publishers, Stanford University Press. © Copyright 1960 by the Board of Trustees of the Leland Stanford Junior University.

and fought for Italian unity, not even drawing back at the seizure of Rome in 1870; the most distinguished of them, Count Alessandro Manzoni, was a senator of the kingdom and had voted to make Rome its capital. Officials of the Catholic Congresses were widely resented for their arrogance; these "bishops in tall hats" were especially disliked by some of the Italian prelates.

Italian bishops were often less intransigent than their parish priests. Bishops had to be acceptable to the royal government before they could take possession of their sees. Therefore the Pope tended to nominate clerics of a moderate cast of mind, compromisers with the new order. Though the theoretical divorce between Church and State in Italy was complete, there was at least in this matter an unspoken practical understanding.

Between 1882, when the suffrage was broadened, and 1888 many Catholic landowners and nobles called for the formation of a "national" Catholic conservative party. But in 1888 relations between the Holy See and the Italian State, still embittered by the Roman Question, suddenly took a turn for the worse. Far from allowing the formation of a Catholic conservative party, which would strengthen the Italian State, the Vatican favored intransigent opposition to Italian Liberalism and the organization of the Italian Catholic masses, socially and economically, *outside* of the Italian political system.

The crisis of the 1890's made both intransigent and conciliatorist positions seem irrelevant to the new situation of Italian Catholics. Leo XIII's *Rerum Novarum* (1891) marks in many ways the beginning of a new course in the Vatican's policy and a new direction to be imparted to the various Catholic movements of Europe. In his declining years the great pontiff turned away from some of the diplomatic maneuvers that had profited the Holy See so little; the Roman Question gave way to the Social Question. The Church's true strength was seen as lying in the Catholic

masses, not in the making of concordats and exchanging of envoys. The new Italian State was by now anchored in the European system, and all hopes of intervention by some Catholic power or powers were futile.

By 1898 the Clericals' intransigent opposition to the State had in fact put them in seeming alliance with the Extreme Left, and the repressions of May struck at both forms of "subversion." This was an absurd and dangerous situation for Italian Catholics. . . . Intransigent opposition to the Italian State no longer fitted the purposes of the Holy See; a settlement of the Roman Question could wait, if necessary, but the menace of the anti-Clerical Left was immediate.

Therefore, after 1898 the Italian militant Catholic movement took a new turn. It had begun on an intransigent base, emphasizing political separateness, but it now developed along more conciliatory lines, attaching greater importance to the social and economic organization of the Catholic masses within the existing state system. The polemic between intransigents and conciliatorists faded away in the early twentieth century, as other issues came to the fore.

Catholics had to face an immediate problem: whether or not to vote. The Holy See had forbidden them to vote in national elections; originally a counsel (*non expedit*), under Leo XIII it hardened into a prohibition. As long as suffrage was restricted to men of means, as in the first years of the new State, this electoral boycott was not important, for the constitutional Liberals had the situation in hand. But the broadening of the franchise, with the rise of revolutionary and irreligious mass parties, made Catholic abstention seem outdated and dangerous. Catholic abstention was part of the nineteenth-century conflict between the Church and the Italian Liberal State: Now that the worst of the conflict was over, why go on abstaining? In municipal elections conservative, "moderate" Catholics freely joined with

the Liberals to shut out the left; why not on a national scale? If, on the other hand, militant Catholicism were regarded as a force of reform rather than as a mere conservative auxiliary, why not use the vote to further Catholic social aims?

While militant Catholics of different tendencies often agreed that it was necessary to take an active part in the political life of the nation, there was no agreement on how this was to be done. All during the stormy period 1898–1900, and until Pius X imposed a temporary solution in 1904, the problem of political participation was an apple of discord; in the varying answers put forth, all the tendencies that have been at work ever since within the Italian Catholic movement may be distinguished, at least embryonically. . . .

Acquiescence or Reconciliation?

After decades the bitter strife between church and state abated in the opening years of the new century. Is it possible to speak of a settlement of differences or rather simply of establishing a *modus vivendi* through acquiescence? Two selections summarizing and evaluating the conflict help provide an answer. One is by the distinguished Italian historian and philosopher Benedetto Croce, the other by Professor Denis Mack Smith of Cambridge University, who has recently published probably the best single volume history of modern Italy.

Tacit Agreement of Church and State

BENEDETTO CROCE

A T the beginning of 1871 only one of the great international questions still remained open — that of the relations between the Kingdom of Italy and the Papacy. In this question almost all the other powers were more or less concerned; and Italy could not refuse to listen to their opinions as to whether the Pope was to be left with little liberty or with much; for the much might prove too much, and the little too little, in view of the relations of the various powers with this peculiar international institution, which was nothing else than the survivor of the ancient Roman Empire, transformed into a spiritual empire or theocracy. The Italian Government was aware of the reality of the problem, and was ready to deal with it by an international arrangement, even to some extent anticipating the thoughts of the parties concerned. But when the various powers, either because they were occupied with other matters or because they fought shy of the difficulties in which they would be involved, showed no desire to accept this spontaneous offer, the Italian Government let it drop amid a general silence, and dealt with the question by means of an internal settlement, a method more in conformity with the idea of a modern state, and with the dignity of Italy. Thus arose the Law of Guarantees (13 May 1871), that is the first part of it. This pronounced the person of the Pope to be sacred and

Benedetto Croce, *A History of Italy 1871–1915*, trans. Cecilia M. Ady (Oxford: Oxford University Press, 1929), pp. 31–34; 65–69. Reprinted by permission of Clarendon Press, Oxford.

inviolable, and granted him royal honours and prerogatives; it guaranteed him full liberty in the exercise of his religious functions and in intercourse with Catholics throughout the world, with special postal and telegraphic facilities; it conceded to representatives of foreign powers at the Vatican diplomatic rights and immunities; it secured to the Pope an annual income out of the revenues of the Italian State, such as he had formerly received from the States of the Church, and left him in enjoyment of the Vatican and of other palaces and villas, and with direct control of the seminaries and other Catholic institutions in Rome, which were exempted from inspection by the Italian education authorities. The law was not drawn up in agreement with the Pope nor accepted by him. He preferred that, from his side, it should retain the character of a hostile edict, imposed by a brutal and treacherous conqueror. This allowed him to pose, in the eyes of Catholics throughout the world, as 'the prisoner of the Vatican,' but it also troubled many Italians, liberal Catholics and moderate, conciliatory, or far-sighted liberals. There were, however, even among men of understanding, sentimentalists and dreamers who, having once hoped that Pius IX would yield to the persuasions of Victor Emmanuel, before the breach was made at Porta Pia, now indulged in daydreams of the entry of the King into Rome and the old Pope going out to meet him, blessing him and embracing him, and blessing and embracing Italy with him and in him, amid a flood of sympathetic tears. With men such as these the desire for 'conciliation' persisted, in the form in which it had been conceived and sought after by Cavour and others, when it was necessary to try to work on these lines in order to secure the co-operation and support of France. On several occasions after 1870, when there was no longer need for any such political bargain, the idea took wings again, and burst out in plans and proposals. But, for the most part, common-sense soon made it plain that this conciliation, which was based on cutting out morsels of territory to make a toy temporal dominion for the Papacy, was as little consonant with the papal dignity as it was with that of Italy. Moreover, for the Papacy, an international political institution, it was impolitic and even impossible to come to an agreement on these lines, for fear of increasing in the eyes of the world its already conspicuously Italian character; it behoved it, rather, to assume the role of one who has yielded to force, of the down-trodden victim, and to continue to protest, at first angrily and later less angrily but no less insistently, never abandoning the assertion of its violated rights. Thus, little by little, the Pope was allowed to have his say unheeded, and his protests were no longer either discussed or answered; clear-sighted Italians realized that, in his place, they could not have acted otherwise, and saw in him an Italian like themselves, as practical and as diplomatically minded as they. It had needed the great upheaval of the wars of the Republic and of the Empire to procure the renunciation of much smaller things, such as Avignon and the County of Venaissin, or the palfrey presented by the Kings of Naples in homage to their over-lord. The failure to come to an agreement in the matter of the temporal power caused distress to the minds of a few loyal citizens and practising Catholics, but, in the general trend of Italian society, too much else caused or might have caused distress to such as these; and even with them the question was not among the most serious, for all more or less realized that the independence of the Papacy would not be increased by the possession of Rome, which had never in the past been an effective source of its greatness. The conclaves which met in Rome all took place without a sign of disturbance, without any hostile demonstration, without even ill-will among the spectators, and this from the first, when, owing to the novelty of the situation, greater precautions were taken. Later conclaves became ordinary events to which little attention was paid, and which were regarded in the same way in which every other nation regarded them. With respect to foreign powers, the unforeseen occurred, but it might nevertheless have been foreseen. The only time that the independence of the Papacy came up for discussion was when Bismarck, at the height of his *Kulturkampf*, was filled with impotent fury at not being able to send a warship to Civitavecchia and to threaten the Pope with bombardment. He sent his remonstrances to the Italian Government, with the only result that he presented the champions of Italy with a first-rate argument in their favour, providing them as he did with a proof that never before had the Papacy been so free. How could the Italians restrain the Pope's verbal extravagances directed against Germany and her Chancellor, if they could not restrain them when they were aimed at themselves? Was it not wiser to suffer them in patience? This was not the opinion of every one, for there were those who cried: 'Down with the Guarantees!' or proposed to tighten the chains which held the Papacy after the death of Pius IX, an event which could not long be delayed. Nevertheless, such was the attitude steadily maintained by the ruling and responsible classes and supported by public opinion. True it is that the failure to bring about a reconciliation, and the way in which the position of the Papacy had been controlled, left Italy with a joint in her armour, vulnerable at times of international tension or war; but until time had covered it with her protecting shield, Italy's only remedy lay in defending herself against attack and conquering in war; and, for the rest, there are joints in the armour of every nation.

. . . It seems at first sight strange that in Italy, the home of the Papacy and once the centre of the counter-reformation and the Catholic reaction, the liberal party could not have found themselves confronted by a Catholic and clerical party, and that the struggle between them should not have taken the foremost place, domi-

nating and overriding all others. It was not that Italy was not in large measure Catholic, including many who took part in public life, together with a few influential statesmen; but the overthrow of the temporal power, and the consequent attitude which the Pope had been obliged to adopt, prevented the formation of a Catholic party which could enter the parliamentary arena. An attempt to form a liberal Catholic association in 1879 was unsuccessful, and moreover, the Vatican opposed any revival of neo-Guelfism. The breach between Church and State, between religious and civil obligations, which this situation seemed to foster, had given, and still gave, much food for thought to men of great moral weight, and more than one method of solving the problem was put forward. . . .

The ruling class in Italy chose the way marked out by Cavour, of 'the free Church in the free State.' This formula became the subject of learned censures, as if it were a formula of thought or a criterion of historical interpretation, whereas it was simply a political formula, and like all political formulas contingent, that is, adapted to existing conditions in Italy and to the character of the Italian people. Nevertheless, criticisms of a political nature were brought to bear upon it. It was suggested that the freedom granted to the Church might prove a formidable weapon, which she would wield with perennial hostility against the Italian State, first by means of teaching, preaching, and the confessional, and secondly by sending her well-disciplined phalanxes to the polls and to Parliament whenever she pleased. . . . To meet the first danger the régime of freedom, or separation, was modified in practice by the retention by the State of certain jurisdictional expedients, such as the *placet* and *exequatur,* and this notwithstanding their abolition in principle by the Law of Guarantees. The principle, however, had not been made applicable to the numerous churches in Crown patronage, and its application was also conditional on the redistribution of ecclesiastical revenues which had not yet been carried out. Hence there were cases of expulsion of bishops and archbishops for having failed to obtain civil recognition by the exequatur, and the new penal code laid down penalties for priests who incited people to disobey the law or refused the sacraments on other than spiritual grounds. As to the other danger, for the time being the Catholic Church kept the faithful from participating in elections or parliaments by means of the *Non expedit* of 1874 [originally issued in 1868 and ostentatiously reaffirmed in 1874] and the principle of 'neither electors nor elected.' If this served the interests of the Papacy in its relations with foreign Catholics, it also served the interests of Italy, which gained a breathing-space in which to establish the lay government so firmly that there was no need to fear the onslaught of the Church's phalanxes when later they decided to enter the arena. Herein lies another instance of the common interests and tacit agreement existing between Italy and the Papacy amid all the noise and abuse and counter-abuse which they were forced to employ against each other on the stage of the world. The thing was so obvious that not only were the politicians aware of it, but it was a matter of common knowledge. In 1874 the Crown Prince Humbert disclosed an open secret when he said to Gregorovius: 'The irreconcilability of the Curia is fortunate for Italy, because it allows the system to mature which will conduce to the healing of the quarrel.' In this quarrel the part of Italian liberalism was to avoid provoking a war of religion by irritating and outraging the Catholic sentiment of the people, and to secure fair play for the clericals, at the same time not neglecting to carry out such reforms as seemed to be demanded in the interests of civil society. Thus came about the confiscation of ecclesiastical property, the suppression of theological faculties in the universities and of spiritual directors in the schools, the reform of charities, the inspection of Catholic schools, the power given to parents in 1877 of asking or refusing doctrinal instruction for their children in the elementary schools, the rendering obligatory of civil marriage, the abolition of religious rites in oath-taking and the like. It was impossible to prevent certain violently anti-clerical or openly anti-religious demonstrations, both from respect for the principle of liberty of thought, and as a means of letting off steam and counteracting the no less violent demonstrations of the Pope and the clericals. . . . On the other hand, no attention was paid to the suggestion that the second part of the Law of Guarantees should be abolished, or limited, or revised, while the first part should be retained unaltered. Persecution of the clericals was not welcomed: isolated experiments in the popular election of parish priests were not encouraged. A divorce law, which perhaps conflicted with the strong family feeling of the Italians, but which was in far greater conflict with Catholic sentiment, was proposed in 1881, 1884, and again in 1902; but although it was sent to parliamentary commissions for examination, it was never passed. In spite of pressure and schemes emanating from the ecclesiastical party, from Audisio in 1876, Curci in 1878, and Tosti in 1887, and in spite of a certain wish for a settlement on the part of statesmen, 'reconciliation,' not only as regards the temporal power but as a whole, was never seriously sought or desired, and in 1886 Spaventa made a memorable speech against the project. Foreigners not deeply versed in Italian affairs imagined that religious war was kindling and fomenting in Italy and might at any moment break out; they deplored her failure to win religious peace and pronounced that this could only be attained by a complete break with Catholicism. But, in truth, Italy was never further removed from wars of religion than when it seemed as if war had been declared by the Papacy. The path of lay and civil development was never easier; so much so that anti-clericalism, with its unnecessary methods of defence and attack, aroused annoyance, and was looked upon as a sign of vulgarity and lack of intelligence. Every one recognized that even if Rome, which had now become a great modern city with a large population and modern interests, were restored to the Pope, he would not know what to do with it, and would promptly have asked Italy to take it back again. At the same time it was realized that the inevitable progress of thought cannot be stemmed by prohibitions, and that in the meantime the dead must be allowed to bury their dead.

Reconciliation of Church and State

DENIS MACK SMITH

Papal hostility had been such that it was rare after 1870 for any leading minister of the Crown to be a devout Catholic: Crispi had called himself a deist, and the Freemasons claimed such names as Depretis, De Sanctis, Spaventa, Di Rudini, Crispi, Cavallotti, Carducci, and even the king himself. The policy of such men had reflected an instinctive prejudice against a Church which was a state within the state. The Church claimed jurisdiction in mixed matters, arbitral authority over all moral issues, and the supremacy of its own law over that of the nation. For sixty years it refused to recognize the very existence of an Italian state, let alone the occupation of Rome.

The Martinucci case of 1882 had decided that, the Pope apart, every inhabitant of the Vatican might be held subject to the Italian courts. Though the crucifix still hung in lecture rooms, an anticlerical minister in 1881 appointed the heretical ex-canon of Mantua, Ardigò, to a professorial chair at Padua, and religious seminaries were threatened with closure if they refused to permit government inspection; in the universities, theological faculties had already been suppressed before the accession to power of the Left. A decree of 1888 put the onus on parents to ask religious education for their children, instead of having to request exemption from it. Then Zanardelli's penal code of 1889 increased the penalties on clergy who condemned from the pulpit existing institutions or acts of the government.

After much opposition, the compulsory payment of tithe was abolished, and most of the remaining church charities were taken over by the state in 1890. This last was a great blow to the clergy, who had obtained much influence from the distribution of alms and doles. Crispi asserted on this occasion that there were 9,464 pious fraternities with a total revenue of nine million lire a year, a sum of which only one-tenth had been devoted as originally intended to public assistance, the rest being spent on masses, candles, and fireworks on gala occasions. Finally, and most wounding of all, in 1895 Crispi made an annual public holiday of September 20, the day on which the royal army in 1870 had turned its cannon against the walls of Rome.

Such measures were anticlerical rather than anti-Catholic; they were, indeed, supported by many sincere Catholics who recognized that Cavour's ideal of "a free Church in a free state" had been repudiated by Rome and was now effectively replaced in liberal dogma by Luzzatti's more realistic formula, "a free Church in a sovereign state." By 1900 the controversy be-

From *Italy, A Modern History*, pp. 222–226, by Denis Mack Smith by permission of the University of Michigan Press. Copyright © by the University of Michigan, 1959.

tween Church and state was looking more and more unreal. Liberalism might be condemned and its products placed on the *Index,* and Catholic protests were heard even against King Umberto's burial in the Pantheon, but the lay state was now untroubled by such censure. In May 1904 Giolitti laid down that "Church and state are two parallel lines which ought never to meet."

Even Popes had to recognize that they had been less disturbed by outside pressure since the loss of temporal power, and the eighty-six encyclicals of Leo XIII had been called collectively the most important contribution to Catholic doctrine since the Middle Ages. The verbal *non possumus* having saved honor, good sense was always at hand to make a compromise in practice. The Pope had been forced to allow bishops to ask for the royal exequatur, just as he had to endure the statue of Garibaldi looking down provocatively from the Janiculum onto the few remaining acres of papal territory. On the other hand, monasteries had been re-endowed since the dissolution, and the census figures of 1881 and 1901 show that, in defiance of formal law, monks and friars increased in number from 7,191 to 7,792, and nuns from 28,172 to 40,251. Sella in the 1870's had been able to say that "the black International is far more dangerous to our liberties than the red," but by 1900 this fear seemed ridiculous. Both sides were developing a mutual tolerance, and the danger of red revolution was giving them a point in common. . . .

In the turmoil of 1898, Christian-democrat groups were formed which — to the concern of the Vatican — did not scorn alliance with the *estrema.* Other Catholics were busy organizing agricultural unions, co-operative dairies, and village banks. . . .

Parallel with this political movement, there were certain kindred heresies . . . which collectively earned from their orthodox ecclesiastical opponents the generic label of "modernism." The modernists sug-

gested that dogma was not to be formulated once and for all, but could be expected to grow organically and change to suit the times. This suggestion, with all its complex of associated ideas, was condemned outright by a new papal syllabus in 1907, though the accused denied many of the beliefs attributed to them. The chief enemy of modernism was Pius X, who reigned from 1903 to 1914 and who was the first Pope of modern times to be canonized—it is interesting that he was elected Pope only after Austria had vetoed the election of the pro-French cardinal Rampolla. Pius felt obliged to protest against the growing materialism and positivism of the age and against the false logic which might lead through modernism to Protestant heresy. Even Fogazzaro, the most popular novelist of the day and a Catholic, had his study in religious psychology, *Il Santo,* placed on the index of prohibited books.

Fifty years earlier the state might have risen to the rescue of a minority within the Church, but Croce and the liberal anticlericals were by now indifferent, and admitted that the Church should regulate itself as it wished. Furthermore, while the Vatican was careful to distinguish what it thought incorrigibly erroneous, it was gradually becoming reconciled to the prevalent trends in modern society. Once the heat of controversy had passed, the Church throughout its history has managed to come to terms with all manner of diverse philosophical and political beliefs, wisely acting to moderate the more extreme views, and warning against irresponsible flirtation with the latest fashionable craze. Its gradual and partial reconciliation with the ideals of liberal democracy was to help Giolitti bring Catholics more actively into political life.

Many churchmen were beginning to conclude that their policy of non-co-operation since 1870 had been quite ineffective. The Vatican had made a grave effort to challenge the secular state and prevent it from taking permanent shape, but with every year that passed success became less likely. Church abstention from politics had hurt no one but the conservatives, and co-operation might be by now, if not a positive good, at least a lesser evil. There was a need for Catholics to appear in parliament and present the church's views on marriage and education, especially when the year 1904 saw the shocking fact of a world congress of freethinkers in the Holy City itself. The new king was accused of atheism — it was said that the only church he built was the Jewish synagogue at Rome — and in February 1902 the speech from the throne had announced another of Zanardelli's projects for permitting divorce. This called for urgent political action in reply. Moreover, the black nobility could not be expected to refuse Court invitations forever, and from contemporary fiction one can see that they and other Catholics were inevitably coming around to take their share in national life. Far from being the enemies of the new state, many Catholics were beginning to think of themselves as its defenders, alike against socialism on the Left and the parallel anticlericalism of Sonnino and Di Rudini on the Right.

Giolitti, though personally favorable to the idea of divorce, was too realistic to antagonize Catholicism directly, and when his plans for socialist support fell through he gladly welcomed as an alternative this other nonconformist faction at the opposite extreme. The election campaign of November 1904 was first opened on a liberal platform, but when the results of the first ballot proved disappointing, Giolitti made positive overtures to the Catholics. It was a novel sight to find the Roman aristocracy haranguing the crowds. *Avanti* calculated afterward that the clerical vote caused the defeat of socialist candidates in twenty-six districts. Then, in June 1905, the encyclical *Il fermo proposito* allowed each bishop to decide whether the Catholics of his diocese might participate in political life, for the recent rupture between the Vatican and France made reconciliation with Italy the more desirable.

III. THE *KULTURKAMPF*: CHURCH AND STATE IN UNITED GERMANY

Aside from those already mentioned in the introduction, other problems resulting from the Vatican Council soon began to appear in Germany. Some priests in charge of parishes, teachers at universities and schools refused to subscribe to the doctrine of Papal Infallibility. Among them was Professor Döllinger, the most famous Catholic church historian of the day. The church excommunicated Döllinger, and demanded that he be removed from the faculty of the University of Munich. The Bavarian king, in the interest of academic freedom and of his right to appoint faculty members, refused to do so. Döllinger's colleagues responded by electing him rector-magnificus of the University. He later helped to organize the Catholics who refused to accept Papal Infallibility and soon the Old Catholic Church with its own bishop came into being. The State was now faced with all sorts of problems. Were these Old Catholics still Catholics? Were they entitled to state support? Could they keep the church property where whole parishes refused to accept infallibility, or must this property be surrendered to the bishop of the diocese?

The Prussian government was faced by the same problems as Bavaria. The Church demanded the dismissal of some professors at Bonn, which was refused. Some of the teachers of religion at Gymnasiums also refused to accept infallibility. A certain Dr. Wollmann in the Polish territories refused to accept the doctrine. The Bishop of the diocese demanded his dismissal and withdrew some pupils of a Catholic institution from the religious classes at the gymnasium. The Prussian Education Minister said the man was teaching exactly what he had always taught in his religion classes and refused to dismiss the teacher. Long memorandums were written and submitted to the king. The state held fast. Obviously some solution would have to be reached. Henceforth would there be Catholic, Old Catholic, and Protestant schools to deal with? In 1841 separate bureaus for Catholic and for Protestant schools had been established in the Ministry of Education. The Prussian government after long deliberation abolished these bureaus on July 8, 1871, much to the dismay and consternation of Catholics. This was followed in March 1872 by a law which brought all schools under state inspection. Formerly clergy had regularly acted as school inspectors; now they had to receive special appointment. In practice Catholic priests were not appointed, especially in the Polish districts, while Protestant clergy continued to be commissioned as state school inspectors.

A brief summary of the most important legislation will point up the nature of the ensuing conflict. There were only three laws passed on the national level. One was the so-called Pulpit Paragraph of November 28, 1871, which was an addition to the Penal Code and forbade the clergy in their official capacity to deal with political matters. Another was a law of June 11, 1872, which excluded the Jesuits and certain related orders from Germany. On February 6, 1875 civil marriage was made obligatory for the empire. In Baden, Hesse, Bavaria, and above all in Prussia, the legislatures passed additional laws. In some states, such as Saxony, Oldenburg, Württemberg, and in the more predominantly Protestant northern states there was little or no controversy. The conflict was most acute in Prussia, where under a new Minister of Culture the so-called Falk laws of 1873 and 1874 were passed. They provided that clergy must receive their education at a German University or approved seminary and must pass an examination in Philosophy, Literature and History. Laws were passed giving the state control of church disciplinary measures, and requiring bishops to submit the names of appointments to parishes to local district government officials. Church officials refused to comply with this last law with the result that bishops were arrested and parishes became vacant. At the height of the conflict out of 4,604 Catholic parishes in

58

Prussia, numbering 8,800,000 souls, 1,103 with 2,085,000 souls were without regular pastoral care. Prussia in 1875 dissolved all monastic orders except those caring for the sick, and also enacted the so-called Bread Basket law, which stopped subsidies to bishops and priests who refused to obey the laws. The articles of the Prussian constitution which guaranteed autonomous government to the churches, and which had previously been amended were cancelled. The state now had no constitutional restrictions on its regulatory legislation.

The Course of the *Kulturkampf*

ERICH EYCK

The first and most active phase of the *Kulturkampf* extended from 1871 to 1876, then there was a period of more or less stagnation to July, 1880, with the concluding phase extending to 1887. It is primarily the first phase with which Professor Erich Eyck, distinguished historian of Modern Germany and biographer of Bismarck, is concerned in the following selection.

THE name *Kulturkampf* (cultural struggle) was given to the great campaign which Bismarck and German Liberalism fought against the Roman Catholic Church and the Catholic Party of the Centrum. In Germany this struggle dominated the minds of men for four or five years and was looked on by a great part of Europe as one of the most exciting events of the age. To-day the questions which then excited so much feeling have receded so far into the background that it is most difficult for us to understand the excitement. But there can be no doubt that in those years many of the most enlightened and highly educated men believed that the future of mankind was at stake.

If we are to try and understand this excitement, we must go back to two acts of the Roman Catholic Church, the publication of the Syllabus of 1864 and the Vatican Decree of Papal Infallibility of 1870.

The *Syllabus errorum*, or "Catalogue of the Principal Errors of our Time", was published by Pope Pius IX in his *Encyclical Quanta Cura*. It contains a list of all the modern doctrines which the Pope reproves, proscribes, and condemns. Now, in this list are to be found almost all the doctrines which Liberalism considers as fundamentals of the state and of modern civilization, and the syllabus was therefore considered a challenge to liberalism and modern culture.

Greater still was the stir caused when the Vatican Council adopted, in June 1870, the dogma of the infallibility of the Pope. Excitement was particularly strong in Germany — which nation considered itself the birthplace of the Reformation — because the majority of the German bishops had opposed this dogma during the Council, but submitted to it according to the fundamental doctrine of the Catholic Church after it had been accepted by the Council. Only a minority of them refused to subscribe to it, and among these was

Reprinted with permission of The Macmillan Company and George Allen & Unwin Ltd. from *Bismarck and the German Empire* by Erich Eyck (London, 1950), pp. 202–211. Copyright 1958 by George Allen & Unwin Ltd.

Dr. Döllinger, a friend of Gladstone and Lord Acton, who was considered the leading light of Catholic theology, and the greatest of German ecclesiastical historians. One section of the opposition organized the Old-Catholic (*Alt-Katholische*) Church to which many contemporaries pinned their greatest hopes, but which, in fact, never grew strong enough to be of real importance.

We need not enter here into doctrinal controversies, but only describe the impression which these events made on the contemporary world. The political importance attached to them is clearly shown — to quote but one example — in Gladstone's pamphlet: *The Vatican Decrees in their Bearing on Civil Allegiance.* If a man of such liberal and tolerant views as Gladstone feared that by these decrees the relations between Church and State were fundamentally changed and the allegiance of devout English Catholics to the state was endangered, we can understand the unrest which they provoked.

At the outset Bismarck was not greatly troubled by the dogma of Infallibility. During the Council he had adopted a rather reserved attitude, even though the Prussian Ambassador at the Holy See, Count Harry Arnim, had advised a more active policy. Bismarck rightly pointed out that Prussia, considered by the Pope as a Protestant Power, could not take the initiative in the affairs of the Catholic Church. But he was willing to follow the initiative of Catholic Powers like Austria or France. When the Council adopted the dogma of Infallibility, the French war had broken out. Bismarck's first concern was to prevent international troubles which could make his task still more difficult. But after the Pope's temporal power had vanished and the Kingdom of Italy had absorbed the Papal State (in September 1870), one of the leading Prussian bishops appeared at the German headquarters in Versailles. This was the Archbishop of Posen, Count von Ledochowsky, whom Bismarck had helped to install in Prussia's Polish provinces and whom he favoured because he saw in him a valuable help in their Germanization, even though he was a Jesuit. Ledochowsky came to Versailles with a twofold request to Bismarck: that he would protest against the destruction of the Papal State and that he would offer the Pope asylum in Prussia if and when he decided to leave Rome. The first plea Bismarck was bound to decline, because it was not in Germany's interest to fall out with the Kingdom of Italy. But he was quite ready to comply with the second, for he felt that, if the Pope resided in Germany, the country's influence would grow; moreover, a Pope within the Fatherland would be a valuable aid to government in home politics.

Here we are face to face with something of the utmost importance for an understanding of Bismarck's attitude. From the very beginning of his administration he had repeatedly asked the Pope to put in a word in his favour with the Prussian Catholics who sat in parliament. He was quite willing to help the Pope in international affairs provided that the Pope arranged for the Catholic deputies to vote for the government. While Ledochowsky was in Versailles, Bismarck said: "If we give asylum to the Pope, he must do something for us in return." And again in conversation with friends he said: "The opposition of the ultramontane clerical party would be checked."

This was all the more important, as a strong ultramontane party was founded just at this time. There had always been a Catholic party in the Prussian Chamber of Deputies, but it had been comparatively weak. The new party which styled itself the "Centre" was much stronger. About seventy "Centre" deputies were returned to the first German Reichstag in 1871. It was, from the outset, the second strongest party. More important perhaps than its size was the fact that it had a first-class political leader in the person of Ludwig Windthorst.

Windthorst was a Hanoverian like the National Liberal leaders Bennigsen and

Miquel, but he remained loyal to his former King after he had lost his throne. Bismarck looked on him as a Guelph and particularist, and cordially detested him. There is a very characteristic saying of Bismarck: "Everyone needs somebody to love and somebody to hate. I have my wife to love and Windthorst to hate." It is very doubtful whether Windthorst returned the compliment. He was much too cool and level-headed to hate an enemy whose greatness he could not fail to appreciate. But this in no wise affected the energy of his opposition. He was not a great orator, but he nearly always knew what to say and how to say it. He kept his temper when Bismarck lost his, and was always ready with an answer. He was an admirable parliamentary tactician, perhaps the best the Reichstag has ever known. As a man he was gentle and civil in manner and of a humane disposition. Although as the foremost champion of Catholicism he was hated by the great mass of the Protestant and Liberal population, he was held in high respect by all members of parliament, however strongly they were opposed to his views and his party.

Bismarck at first tried to induce the Pope to come out against the Centre Party, and the Cardinal Secretary of State, Antonelli, did, in fact, utter a few words which could be interpreted in this sense and which Bismarck hastened to make public. But, of course, it was easier still for the leaders of the Catholic Centre to get the ear of Rome, and they induced Antonelli to make another statement which put paid to all hopes of a breach between the Papal *curia* and the Centre Party.

Bismarck now went over to the offensive. In an article (19th June 1871) in the Conservative *Kreuz-Zeitung* he declared war on the Centre, and a few weeks later he abolished the Catholic Department of the Prussian *Kultus-Ministerium*. In January 1872, when the deputies of the Centre Party questioned Bismarck in the Chamber about this step, the Chancellor replied with a vehement attack on the party. He called its formation a mobilization against the state and taxed Windthorst with not welcoming the foundation of the German Empire. He even tried to brand him as *Reichsfeind*, that is, an enemy of the Empire. Windthorst answered: "The Chancellor is not the State. Until now no minister has been so presumptuous as to call his opponents enemies of the state." This was, indeed, Bismarck's method. All the parties who opposed him were called *Reichsfeinde*. This was a new kind of proscription proclaimed by the formidable head of the government and repeated by hundreds of newspapers. It is by this means that venom and bitterness were instilled into public life in Germany.

From now on it was open warfare between Bismarck and the Centre Party as the political champion of the Catholic Church in Germany. In this struggle the great majority of the non-Catholic population, that is, about two-thirds of the country, was wholeheartedly on Bismarck's side. Many of them felt that this battle was being waged to uphold modern culture against the onslaughts of obscurantism. The term *Kulturkampf* was coined by the great pathologist, Professor Rudolf Virchow of Berlin, a Progressive member of parliament and by no means a blind devotee of Bismarckian power politics. He and his friends hoped that this struggle would free the schools from clerical influence, both Catholic and Protestant. Other more conservative politicians thought that the struggle was necessary to maintain the rights of the state. The particular bugbears of the Protestants were the members of the Society of Jesus, the Jesuits, who were looked on as extremely sly and cunning intriguers. In 1872 the Reichstag approved an anti-Jesuit measure which gave the government the right not only to dissolve all sections of the Society of Jesus, but to banish all its members from the country. This was an exceptional law of the very worst type, a negation of the fundamental liberal principle of civic equality and freedom of worship and conscience. Nevertheless, not only the Conservatives but the great majority of the Liberals voted for it. Some of the foremost Liberals were its principal sponsors. The honour of Liberalism was only saved by Lasker who, in spite of his party's vehemence, declared that his conscience. compelled him to vote against so illiberal a measure.

The major battles were fought out in the Prussian Landtag. The administration of schools and churches belonged not to the Empire but to the individual states — Prussia, Bavaria, and the rest. Bismarck considered the existing Prussian laws insufficient to maintain the authority of the State against the Church militant. New legislation was necessary. For this task he required a new *Kultus-Minister*. For this post he secured Adalbert Falk, a high official in the Ministry of Justice. When he was offered the post, Falk asked the Chancellor: "What am I expected to do?" Bismarck answered: "To re-establish the rights of the State in relation to the Church, and *with as little fuss as possible.*" But in this latter respect no one sinned more than Bismarck himself. The speeches with which he introduced the new legislation for Prussia caused the greatest possible stir. They are among the most vigorous and vehement he ever made. He attacked the Centre with all his tremendous strength and energy, singling out its leader, Windthorst, for particular attack and trying to loosen the ties between the man and his party. It was, of course, to no purpose whatever. One of the other leaders of the party, von Mallinckrodt, described Windthorst as a pearl to which his party had given the right setting. Windthorst himself answered Bismarck's attack on his leanings to the Hanoverian King with the dignified words: "My loyalty to the Royal family of Hanover will last until my dying day, and nothing in the world, not even the most powerful Chancellor of Germany, will be able to make me depart from it. But I remember the words of the Bible: obey them that have rule over you and

submit yourselves, and I have done my duty as a subject to the best of my conscience." He closed with a sentence which Bismarck had occasion to remember many years later: "It is easy to cling to the monarchical principle in fair weather; it is harder in foul."

In other speeches Bismarck called the Centre Party "a battery against the state," and lumped them together with the Social Democrats when he called them "two parties which opposed national development by international methods and which fought against the nation and the national state."

He made an even greater impression when he characterized his present campaign as a part of the age-old struggle between priest and king, which was older than Christendom, as the example of the conflict between Agamemnon and Calchas in Tauris showed. But what kindled the enthusiasm of the majority of the nation more than all else, was his cry to the Reichstag: "We shall not go to Canossa!" For the fact that the Emperor Henry IV had done penance before Pope Gregory VII in the winter of 1077 was considered the deepest humiliation ever suffered by the old German Empire and the greatest triumph of the Papacy. Thus Bismarck gave the nation the impression that it was involved in an eternal conflict which had brought it much misery and affliction in the past, but which this time would be fought out to a victorious conclusion.

Falk would have needed the dexterity of a conjurer to realize Bismarck's programme without fuss. We cannot go here into the details of his legislative attempts. There is no doubt that in the main he failed. Nevertheless, he is not at all a contemptible figure. He earnestly believed in his task and spared no pains to discharge it. He is, perhaps, alone among all the Ministers a personality whom history will remember, and certainly the only one who achieved popularity in his own right. In one election seven constituencies elected him to the Chamber at the same time. To this very day his name is remembered with gratitude by the elementary school teachers of Prussia, for he did more for them than any Minister before or after. Bismarck himself, who in his reminiscences tries to disclaim all responsibility for Falk's measures, cannot help acknowledging his rare gifts and his never failing courage.

It was not Falk's fault if his measures proved abortive. Bismarck had at least as much to do with it. The trouble was that Bismarck never fully understood the Catholic Church. Odo Russell, the British Ambassador in Berlin, wrote in 1874 that Bismarck and his government were not aware of the power of passive resistance of the Roman Catholic clergy. "The Roman Church has always derived strength from persecution, but it is impotent against the power of freedom and its blessings. . . . Bismarck's anti-church policy has compelled the German bishops to rally round the Pope and to suffer martyrdom for discipline's, obedience's and example's sake."

How little Bismarck understood the nature of the resistance he provoked emerges from a well-known passage in his *Reminiscences.* "The error in the conception of the Prussian laws was made obvious to me by the picture of dexterous, light-footed priests pursued through back doors and bedrooms by honest but awkward Prussian gendarmes, with spurs and trailing sabres." He understood the moral forces which were summoned up against him in the *Kulturkampf* as little as he had understood them in the Prussian constitutional conflict.

The political effect of the *Kulturkampf* was that Bismarck was drawn closer to the Liberals and farther from the Conservatives. The Conservatives did not, as a rule, worry overmuch about the Catholics; only old Ludwig von Gerlach, who was for so many years one of the intellectual leaders of the *Kreuz-Zeitung* and who later broke away from Bismarck over his 1866 policy, now joined the Centre Party and opposed his former friend as a Centre deputy. But the majority of the Conservatives, especially

those of the *Kreuz-Zeitung* school, cared very deeply about the Protestant Church and its influence in education. As Falk's law interfered with the inspection of elementary schools by the clergy of both the Catholic and Protestant Churches, they sat up in opposition and came into sharp conflict with Bismarck. One of Bismarck's oldest friends, Hans von Kleist-Retzow, attacked his policy violently in the Herrenhaus (the Prussian Upper Chamber) and was even more violently rebuked by him. Kleist had reproached Bismarck with breaking away from the Conservative Party. Bismarck answered with biting sarcasm: "The part breaks away from the whole, the mobile from the static; the King and the government have not broken loose from the Conservative party, but the Conservative party from them." At the next election in 1874 he showed the Conservatives that they were powerless without the help of the government. The number of their deputies in Reichstag and Landtag sank as low as it had in the years of the Prussian constitutional conflict. The National Liberals and the Progressives gained, but so did the Centre Party, which approached a hundred seats in both Assemblies.

But the opposition of the Conservatives had a facet to show other than the parliamentary one. The old Emperor sympathized with them in his heart of hearts. In his old age he grew very orthodox in religious matters and he feared that the Protestant Church would be weakened. He none the less appended his signature to the new laws, but with great reluctance. As early as 1874 he said: "The time has come to rule more on Conservative lines." Stronger still was the distaste which the Empress Augusta felt for the *Kulturkampf.* She strongly disapproved of the persecution of the Catholic clergy and understood the Catholic Church much better than Bismarck did. He was aware, of course, of her opposition, and his dislike of Augusta deepened. There is perhaps no person who receives such spiteful mention in his *Reflections and Recollections* as Augusta; he blames her for every set-back in his political career.

The dramatic climax of the *Kulturkampf* was the attempt which Kullmann, a young journeyman cooper, made on Bismarck's life in Kissingen in July 1874. Kullmann was a member of a Catholic working-men's club. The government tried to represent the attempt as the outcome of a Catholic conspiracy, but without success. Bismarck was wounded in the right hand, but only slightly. Nevertheless he took the attempt very seriously. In December 1874 a deputy of the Centre Party, the Bavarian Jörg, in a speech to the Reichstag made a sarcastic allusion to the excitement which the incident had occasioned in the country at large. Bismarck, in reply, made a passionate attack on the Centre Party: "You may try," he cried, "to disown this assassin, but none the less he is clinging to your coat-tails." To be thus accused of complicity in a murderous attack understandably infuriated the Centre deputies, and one of them voiced an angry *"Pfui!"* Shaking with fury, Bismarck retorted: *"Pfui* is an expression of disgust and contempt. Don't imagine these feelings are very far from me either.

The only difference is that I am too polite to voice them." The member who made this notable interruption was Count von Ballestrem, twenty-five years later the highly respected President of the Reichstag. It was he of whom Bismarck said, if he had chanced to have a revolver in his pocket when the remark was made, he would have shot the man who made it.

To read of these passionate and vehement attacks by Bismarck on the Centre Party, one might think that peace between them was utterly out of the question. And, recalling his words about the undying struggle for power between kingdom and priesthood and his defiant declaration never to go to Canossa, one might imagine that Bismarck would never lay aside his sword until the enemy had surrendered unconditionally. But the amazing thing is that he not only broke off the engagement before he won a conclusive victory and annulled most of the measures for which he had so doughtily campaigned, but he also made it up with the Centre Party in order to shake off the National Liberals and undermine their parliamentary position.

Key Documents

Passions ran high during the *Kulturkampf* and nothing reveals this better than some of the original speeches and documents of that period. Here are selected excerpts from some speeches of Bismarck; two statements where the term *Kulturkampf* was first used by Dr. Rudolf Virchow, leader of the Progressive party; an excerpt from the encyclical of Pius IX in which he declared the Prussian anti-clerical laws null and void; and two letters from the Cardinal State Secretary urging the leaders of the Center party to support new army legislation desired by Bismarck, in order to win his favor for the cancellation of anti-clerical measures. (See introductory note to the next section, "Victory, Defeat, or Compromise?") If Germans use long sentences in writing, their style in parliamentary debate is even more involved. Speeches are full of subordinate clauses which repeat and enforce previous points; Bismarck was a master of this technique as these excerpts from his speeches demonstrate.

We Shall Not Go to Canossa

BISMARCK

Excerpts from Bismarck's speech in the Reichstag on the Refusal of the Pope to accept Cardinal Hohenlohe as German Ambassador to the Holy See, May 14, 1872.

The tasks of an embassy consist, on the one hand, in protecting its citizens; on the other hand, however, also in negotiating the political relations between the imperial government and the court to which the ambassador is accredited. Now there is no foreign sovereign, who according to the existing status of our laws would be called upon to exercise such extensive — coming close to sovereignty and unlimited by any constitutional responsibility — rights within the German Reich by virtue of our laws. It is therefore, for the German Reich, of considerable interest how it stands diplomatically in relation to the supreme head of the Roman Church, who exercises an influence among us so exceptionally wide for a foreign sovereign.

I hardly believe that it would be possible for an ambassador of the German Reich, considering the prevailing climate of opinion in the Catholic Church, through the most able diplomacy by persuasion to exert an influence which would achieve a modification of the position his Holiness has taken on similar matters on the basis of principle. I hold that it would be impossible, after the recently pronounced and openly promulgated dogmas of the Catholic Church, for a secular power to conclude a concordat, without this secular power being effaced to a degree and in a way which at least the German Reich cannot accept.

Do not be concerned, we shall not go to Canossa, neither bodily nor spiritually.

But nevertheless no one can deny that the situation of the German Reich in regard to confessional peace is a troubled one. The governments of the German Reich are urgently seeking, seek with the greatest care, which they owe to their Catholic as well as to their Evangelical subjects, for means which will enable them to move from the present condition to a more acceptable one in the most peaceful fashion, while disturbing as little as possible the confessional relationships of the Reich. . . .

I had hoped that through the selection of an ambassador who had the full confidence of both sides, first in respect to his love for truth and his reliability, secondly in respect to his conciliatory views and behaviour, that the selection of such an ambassador as his Majesty the Emperor had hit upon in the person of a well known Prince of the Church would be welcome in Rome, that it would be viewed as a pledge of our peaceful conciliatory frame of mind, that it would be used as a bridge for reconciliation. . . .

Unfortunately, because of reasons which have not yet been presented to us, these intentions of the Imperial Government did not reach fruition, because of a curt refusal on the part of the Papal curia.

My regrets over this refusal are extraordinarily lively. I am however not justified in coloring this regret with touchiness because the government owes it to our Catholic citizens not to grow weary in seeking out the road by which may be found a settlement of the boundary between clerical and secular power (which we absolutely need in the interest of our internal peace)

From Ludwig Hahn, *Geschichte des Kulturkampfes in Preussen in Aktenstücken dargestellt* (Berlin: Verlag Wilhelm Hertz, 1881), pp. 72–74. (Trans. Ernst and Louise Helmreich).

in the most forbearing and, for our confessional relationships, least disturbing way. I will therefore not permit myself to become discouraged by what has happened, but will continue my efforts with His Majesty toward the end that a representative of the Reich will be found for Rome who will enjoy the confidence of both powers, if not in equal degree, at least in sufficient measure for him to carry out his tasks. That this task has been made much more difficult by what has happened, I cannot conceal.

* * *

This I can assure you, contrary to the assertions which some clerical subjects of his Majesty the King of Prussia make to the effect that there can be laws of the land which are not binding on them, that against such assertions we will uphold *the complete undivided sovereignty* with all measures at our command, and that in this attitude we are certain of the full support of the great majority of both confessions.

Sovereignty can only be unitary and it must remain so: the sovereignty of making the law! and he who says that the law of his country is not binding for himself, places himself outside the law and severs himself from the law.

The Kulturkampf, A Struggle for Civilization

DR. RUDOLF VIRCHOW

Excerpts from a speech on the Education and Appointment of Clergy in the Prussian Lower Chamber, January 17, 1873.

. . . We fully acknowledge, that you [the Center party] need not debate with us, that you do not have to remind us that at the time [of the Middle Ages] the Church was indeed the bearer of universal civilization; that we freely recognize. We have at all times given the Church the honor, we have admitted, that there was no province of human thought in which the church at that time did not truly carry all civilization. Inasmuch as you place such substantial significance on these matters, I want especially to stress that the civilization which the church then carried was not the specific Christian civilization of today; (Very true! from the Left) it was rather the universal civilization of mankind. This civilization the ancient pagans likewise taught, made it part of their lives, sanctioned it, as did the church fathers. Aristotle, Plato, Galen were recognized just as much as Augustine and Tertullian. (Interjection from the Center: That is still the case today! Another interjection: But not in Matters of Faith!) Not in matters of faith, certainly. (Laughter) That is exactly it; that they always confuse this. They make out, as if the old church, the true civilizing-church, had reached its position through the dogmatic matters which it had pursued. No, gentlemen, it achieved esteem because it was really the bearer of the whole human development. (Very true! from the Left), not as the bearer of dogmatic development. Gradually through the activity of this civilizing church, through the monasteries, through the monastic schools, through the clergy, secular and regular, it reached a point where a greater number of people shared in learning; where the laity as equal bearers of culture could assert themselves, and,

From *Stenographischer Bericht über die Verhandlungen des Preussischen Landtags, Abgeordnetenhaus,* 28 Sitzung, January 17, 1873, vol. I, pp. 630–631. (Trans. Ernst and Louise Helmreich.)

Gentlemen, from that moment there began not only heresy, but also the one-sided dogmatic development of the church and the Papacy. (Interjection: Arius!)

Yes, Gentlemen, one or another heretic there was earlier, that I admit, only the old heresy was in reality a different one from the new. We certainly don't want here to go into great Conciliar negotiations, but, Gentlemen, it is obvious that the modern heresy, against which you struggle and from the subsequent development of which the history of the world has taken the course which it now follows, and from which eventually the most recent political situations derived, the Italian and then the French War, this heresy is of later date, it dates from the moment when the educated laity came into conflict with the church.

This educated laity it is well known found its most distinguished expression in one of the greatest ruling dynasties of Germany, the Hohenstaufens. It was the great Emperor Frederick II who attempted to nail down humane thought in state forms. The Hohenstaufens succumbed in the bloodiest battles, the hierarchy triumphant; then carried out its further developments, and more and more became accustomed to this specific dogmatic style. But, Gentlemen, likewise from this time on it took on more and more the peculiar character of ultramontanism, as gradually the College of Cardinals was made up of an increasing number of Italians, the Popes ever more exclusively were chosen from Italian bishops, and the Papacy as such presented itself as really an Italian church power. That you certainly will not dispute. (Opposition from the Center).

So? That is, however, the historical development. That is the way we look at the matter, Gentlemen, and I relate it to you not only in order to sparkle with a little piece of erudition, but also because I have the conviction that here it is a question of a great struggle for civilization [es handelt sich hier um einen grossen Kulturkampf]. From this point of view I also approach the consideration of this law. For me it is not a law from today to tomorrow, instead it is a law deriving from the great developments of thousands of years. (Opposition from the Center.)

That this is not the best expression for it, about this I will not quarrel, but an expression it is.

Now, Gentlemen, this Italian Papacy from which ultramontanism has emerged in its modern form, this ultramontane Papacy, has indeed shifted the bases for negotiations between even the most benevolent state and the church, inasmuch as in the Vatican decisions it has won an entirely new and up to now totally unprecedented status. (Opposition from the Center.)

Yes, Gentlemen, more benevolent no state could have been towards Catholicism than Prussia was. (Opposition from the Center.)

Gentlemen at this moment you dispute everything; no matter what a person says, you say "No" (Laughter). . . .

The Program of the Progressive Party

DR. RUDOLF VIRCHOW

Excerpts from the Program of the Progressive Party in the Reichstag Elections, March 23, 1873.

. . . Voters! The great goals which the German Progressive party has sought since its founding have by no means been at-

From Felix Salomon, *Die deutschen Parteiprogramme* (Leipzig and Berlin: Verlag von B. G. Teubner, 1907), vol. II, pp. 12–14. (Trans. Ernst and Louise Helmreich.)

tained. Meanwhile much of it has been realized more swiftly than ever we had dared to hope, and whoever compares the situation of public affairs today with those of twelve years ago will have to admit that the state-sponsored changes are more in accord with our program than those of our opponents.

[After enumerating various accomplishments the program continues.] Finally, also in the field of human and individual development several great steps forward have been taken. The school regulations have fallen. With the decisive cooperation of our party the government has put through the law on school inspection authorities, and in the long row of church laws the definitive break with that objectionable system of mutual insurance between civil servant domination in the state and priest domination in the church, which so long has held down our development, will be confirmed.

There were few of these measures which our party could support without reservation. It tried at the time, to obtain those amendments to the laws which it thought

were desirable. But if indeed it was all too often unsuccessful it has nevertheless recognized the necessity, in company with the other liberal parties, to support the government in a struggle which every day is taking on more of the character of a great struggle for the civilization of mankind [. . . *der mit jedem Tage mehr den Charakter eines grossen Kulturkampfes der Menschheit annimmt*].

The Progressive party because of this has not become a government party. It is a party of independent men, who have no obligations to the government or to its individual members. Its program was and is a purely objective one. . . . Great decisions in the realm of school and church are in prospect; especially it will be decided for a long time ahead if in the future church constitution, the parish will be granted its rightful place. Take care, therefore, through the election of independent and truly free-thinking men, that the decision does not go against freedom, not against education, not against the more noble goals of mankind.

On Kingship and Priesthood

BISMARCK

Excerpts from the Speech of Prince Bismarck in the Prussian Upper Chamber on amending the Church Articles of the Prussian Constitution March 10, 1873.

The problem in which we are involved is in my opinion being falsified, and the light, in which we view it, is a false one, if we consider it as a confessional, a church question. It is essentially political.

It is not a struggle as our Catholic co-citizens are led to believe, of an Evangelical dynasty against the Catholic church,

it is not a struggle between belief and disbelief: it is the age-old struggle for power, that is as old as humanity; the power struggle between Kingship and Priesthood; the power struggle, which is much older than the appearance of our Savior in this world; the power struggle that was with Agamemnon and his seers in Aulis, which cost him his daughter and hindered the departure of the Greeks; the power struggle that dominated German medieval history up to the dissolution of the Empire

From Hahn, *op. cit.*, pp. 118–121. (Trans. Ernst and Louise Helmreich.)

under the name of the struggles of the Popes with the Emperors; which in the Middle Ages came to its end with the death of the last representative of the illustrious Swabian dynasty on the scaffold under the axe of a French conqueror, and this French conqueror was allied with the then reigning Pope.

The papacy has always been a political power that with the greatest decisiveness and with the greatest success has intervened in the affairs of this world, that has sought these opportunities for intervention and made them its program. These programs are known. The goal which the papal power has constantly had in mind; the program, which in the time of the medieval emperors was close to realization, is the subjugation of the secular power to the spiritual, an eminently political purpose, an endeavor which indeed is as old as humanity.

The struggle of priesthood and kingship, the struggle in this case of the Pope with the German emperor, as we have already seen it in the Middle Ages, is to be judged like every other conflict: it has its alliances, it has its conclusions of peace; it has its halting places, it has its armistices. There have been peaceful popes, there have been those bent on fighting and conquest. It has also not always been the case that in the struggles of the Papacy, that it was exactly Catholic powers that were the sole allies of the Pope; also the priests have not always stood on the side of the Pope. We have had cardinals as ministers of great powers at a time when these great powers were carrying through a strong anti-papal policy even by force. We have found bishops contrary to papal interests in the levies of the German emperors.

Thus this struggle for power is subject to the same conditions as every other political struggle, and it is a distortion of the issue, which is intended to influence thoughtless people, when it is represented as if it dealt with the suppression of the church. It has to do with defending the state, it has to do with defining how far

the rule of the priesthood and how far the rule of the king shall go, and this demarcation must be such that the state for its part can exist with it. For in the realm of this world the state has rule and precedence.

Thus the problem is pretty much independent of the confessional one, which I will only mention. In this connection I can mention that it was the through and through strongly Evangelical, one could almost say, in his religious convictions anti-Catholic, King Frederick William III, who at the Congress of Vienna pressed for the restoration of the secular rule of the Pope and successfully carried this through. Nonetheless he was in conflict with the Catholic Church on departing from this world. We then in the constitutional paragraphs which presently concern us found a *modus vivendi,* an armistice, which was concluded at a time when the state felt itself in need of help, and believed this help to be found, at least partially, in a connection with the Catholic Church.

At that time there came into being the *modus vivendi,* under which we have lived in a peaceful relationship for a number of years.

There perhaps has never been a time when, aside from everything else, if the government had not been attacked, we were more inclined to an agreement with the Roman chair than exactly at the close of the French War. It was very unlikely that a preference for Italy would have been of influence on our policy of that period.

But even while we were still in Versailles, it surprised me somewhat that a request was sent to all Catholic members of parliamentary groups to declare themselves, if they were of a mind to join a Confessional party, such as we today know as the Center party, and if they would agree in imperial politics to press and vote for the incorporation of these paragraphs, which we are dealing with today, into the Imperial Constitution. This program at that time did not yet alarm me much —

to that degree did I desire peace — I knew from whom it came, partly from a highly placed prince of the church who, of course, has the obligation to do what he can for papal policy, and in this was fulfilling his obligation; partly from a prominent member of the Center party, the former Prussian representative at the Diet of the Confederation, von Savigny; by these the movement was chiefly introduced. The latter I believed would not use his influence in an anti-government way. I was completely mistaken. I am just mentioning the reasons why I at that time did not attribute importance to this affair, so that I did not return to Germany without being convinced that it would also be possible to live with this party and its aspirations.

When I, however, was here, I first saw how strong the organization of this party of the church which was battling the state had become; what first called my attention to the danger was the power which this newly formed group had won for itself. Representatives of electoral districts who were resident and respected and had long been regularly elected, were now on decree from Berlin removed, and the election of other representatives prescribed whose names were not even known in the electoral districts; this happened not in one but in several electoral districts; they had achieved such a disciplined organization and such control over their minds as was necessary if one wanted to realize the program of the Bishop of Mainz as he announced it in his printed circulars. What was the intent of this program? Look it up. There are circulars ingeniously written and pleasant to read in the hands of everyone; it was a plan to introduce into the Prussian state political dualism by establishing a state within a state, to bring all Catholics to a point where they received guidance for their conduct in political as in private life exclusively from this Center party. By

this we would reach a dualism of the worst kind; it is possible to govern with a dualistic constitution in a country where conditions are favorable; the Austro-Hungarian state shows us this; but there, there is no confessional dualism. Here it is rather a matter of establishing two confessional states, which would stand in a dualistic struggle with each other, of which the highest sovereign of one is a foreign Church-Prince who has his seat in Rome, a Church-Prince who by the recent changes in the constitution of the Catholic church has become mightier than he formerly was; we would have therefore, if this program became a reality, instead of the existing unified Prussian state, instead of the to-be-created German Reich, two state organisms running parallel to each other: the one with its general staff in the Center Party, the other with its general staff in the leading secular principle, and in the government and in the person of his Majesty the Emperor.

This situation was a totally unacceptable one for the government; it was its duty to defend the state against this danger. The whole question is this: are these paragraphs, as the government of His Majesty bears testimony, dangerous to the state or are they not? If they are, then you fulfill your conservative duty if you vote against the retention of these paragraphs. If you hold they are in no way dangerous, then this is a conviction which the government of His Majesty does not share, and it can no longer bear the responsibility of carrying on affairs with these constitutional articles; it must leave this to those who do not consider these paragraphs as dangerous.

In its struggle to defend the State the government turns to the Herrenhaus with the request for support and for help in strengthening the state and in defending it against attacks and subversive actions, which endanger its peace and its future.

Encyclical on the May Laws

PIUS IX

Excerpts from the Encyclical of the Pope to the Archbishops and Bishops of Prussia of February 5, 1875.

What we had never thought possible, recalling the regulations which this Apostolic See agreed upon with the highest governing authority of Prussia in the 21st year of the current century for the welfare and prosperity of the Catholic cause, has come to pass, worthy Brothers, in your territories in the most lamentable way, since upon the repose and peace which the church of God enjoyed among you, a heavy and unexpected storm has descended. For to the laws which have recently been issued against the rights of the church, and which have already hit many devoted and sincere servants of the church, both among the clergy and among believing folk, new ones have been added which completely overthrow the God-given constitution of the church, and entirely destroy the holy prerogatives of the bishops. . . .

[After reviewing some of the laws and referring to bishops who have been imprisoned the encyclical continues.] But even if they [imprisoned bishops] deserve shining words of praise rather than tears of sympathy, nevertheless the degradation of the bishop's office, the infringement of the freedom and rights of the church, the persecutions which weigh down not only those bishoprics named [Gnesen, Posen, Paderborn] but also others in Prussia, demand from us, in accordance with the apostolic office which God, without merit on our part has granted to us, that we raise our voice in protest against these laws

which are the source of those already realized misdeeds and many more yet to be feared, and that we intervene with all decisiveness and with the authority of divine law for the freedom of the church which has been suppressed by Godless authority. In order to fulfill this duty of our office, we openly declare through this letter to all whom it may concern, and to the whole Catholic World that those laws are invalid since they are completely contrary to the God-given institutions of the church. For the Lord has not set the mighty of this earth as superiors to the bishops of his church in those things which concern their holy service, but rather holy Peter who was commissioned not only to feed his lambs but also his sheep (John 21: 16, 17), and therefore by no, be it ever so high-standing, secular power can those be deprived of their bishop's office, whom the Holy Ghost has placed as bishops to rule the church (Acts 20: 28). . . .

It would appear as if these laws were not given to free citizens in order to ask of them a sensible loyalty, but were imposed on slaves, to extort their loyalty through fear of force. This however should not be so understood, as if we believed that those may be rightly excused, who out of fear obeyed man rather than God; no less so than if the Godless men, if there are such, would remain unpunished by the divine judge who, relying solely on the protection of the secular power, have taken over orphaned parish churches and have dared to conduct holy services in them. To the contrary we declare, that these ungodly persons, and all, who in the future by a similar crime have forced themselves

From Hahn, *op. cit.*, pp. 163–166. (Trans. Ernst and Louise Helmreich.)

into the dominion of the church, in accordance with the Holy Canons, legally and truly have fallen and fall under the greater excommunication; and we admonish all the pious faithful that they shall stay away from their services, shall not receive the sacraments from them, and refrain carefully from contact and communication with them, in order that the bad leaven may not spoil the whole. . . .

Vatican Advice to the Central Party

CARDINAL JACOBINI

First Note of the Cardinal State Secretary Jacobini to the Nuncio in Munich January 3, 1887.

Confidential. From my telegram of January 1 you have seen that very soon the draft of the final revision of the Prussian church-political laws. will be presented. Very recently we have had formal assurance in regard to this which confirms the reports which had earlier reached the Holy See. You can consequently put at ease Mr. Windthorst and dispel the doubts which he expressed in his letter which was enclosed in your last esteemed report. In view of this shortly forthcoming revision of the church laws, which we have reason to believe will turn out to be satisfactory, the Holy Father wishes that the Center would support the bill for the Military Septennate by all the means at its disposal. It is indeed well known that the government lays the greatest importance on the acceptance of this law. If it thereby would be possible to dissipate the danger of an immediate war, then the Center would have made itself of great service to the fatherland, to humanity, to Europe. In the opposite case the action of the Center would not escape being considered as unpatriotic and the dissolution of the Reichstag would also cause the Center not inconsiderable embarrassments and uncertainties. Through the support by the Center of the Septennate bill the government would in return become even more inclined to the Catholics and to the Holy See. The Holy See places no small value on the continuance of peaceful and mutually reliable relations with the Berlin government. You should therefore energetically interest the leaders of the Center for this, so that they will use all their influence with their colleagues in accordance with the assurance furnished you, that by agreeing to the Septennate law they would give the Holy Father much joy, that this would be very advantageous for the cause of the Catholics. If the latter as a result of the military laws continue to face new burdens and difficulties, they will on the other hand be compensated by the complete religious peace, which is after all the greatest of all possessions.

In that I intrust the foregoing considerations to your tact and to your circumspection, I am convinced that with consideration of the persons and circumstances involved, you will make use of it.

Second Note of the Cardinal Secretary Jacobini to the Nuncio in Munich January 21, 1887.

Right Reverend Sir! I have received your esteemed letter of the 19th of this month, in which Your Reverence encloses a copy of a letter which Baron von Franckenstein sent to you. While I desist from considering the reasons which the Baron advances

From Ludwig Bergsträsser, *Der politische Katholizismus. Dokumente seines Entwicklung* (2 vols., Munich: Drei Masken Verlag, 1923), vol. II, pp. 140–141. (Trans. Ernst and Louise Helmreich.)
From Bergsträsser, *op. cit.*, pp. 146–148. (Trans. Ernst and Louise Helmreich.)

to justify the actions of the Center in the vote on the Military Septennate, [they had voted against it], I consider it a matter of great urgency and of present interest to turn my attention to the other portions of his letter. He wishes to know if the Holy See believes that the presence of the Center in the Reichstag is no longer needed; in this case he along with the majority of his colleagues would not accept a new mandate. He added, that, as he had already explained in 1880, the Center could not accept directives in regard to laws which did not involve church matters and which did not touch upon the rights of the church. You will take care to assure the Baron that the Holy See constantly recognizes the laurels which the Center and its leaders have won for themselves in the defense of the Catholic cause. After that in the name of the Holy Father you will inform him of the following considerations which are related to his inquiry.

The task of the Catholics to protect their religious interests can by no means be considered exhausted, since a limited and temporary as well as a final and lasting aspect must be recognized. To work towards the complete cancellation of the conflict-laws, to defend the correct interpretation of the new laws and to watch over their implementation, all this demands at all times the activity of Catholics in the Reichstag. In addition one must consider that in a nation, which in religious respects is mixed and in which Protestantism is looked on as the state religion, opportunities for religious friction will be present when Catholics will be called upon to defend their position in legal ways, or to make their influence felt in order to better their own situation. And one must not fail to stress that a parliamentary representation of Catholics, since it interests itself in the unbearable conditions which are prepared for the supreme head of the church, could avail itself of favorable opportunities to express and assert the wishes of the Catholic citizens in favor of the Holy Father. Furthermore the Center, considered as a political party, has always been left full freedom of action; as such it could not itself represent the interests of the Holy See. If, in the matter of the Septennate the Holy Father believed that he should inform the Center of his views on this question, this is to be ascribed to the circumstance that matters of a religious and moral order were tied up with this affair. Above all there was good reason to believe that the final revision of the May laws would be given a strong impulse and would receive thorough consideration by the government if the latter had been satisfied by the action of the Center in voting for the Septennate law. In the second place the cooperation of the Holy See for the maintenance of peace by way of the Center party would have necessarily obligated the Berlin government and would have put it in a more benevolent mood towards the Center and one more indulgent to the Catholics. Finally the Holy See believed in giving advice in regard to the Septennate that a new opportunity had been given it to show the German Emperor and Prince Bismarck a favor. In addition, the Holy See, out of consideration of its own interests which are identical with the interests of Catholics, can not permit any opportunity to pass through which can make the mighty German Empire more inclined to the improvement of the church's position in the future.

The above reflections, which summarize the religious and moral aspects of the Septennate law from the viewpoint of the Holy See influenced the Holy Father to make his wishes known to the Center. Your reverence, when communicating the present letter, which like my last one, presents the sublime thoughts of His Holiness, to Baron von Franckenstein, will instruct him to inform the parliamentary representatives of the Center party.

With the assurance of distinguished esteem, etc.

Victory, Defeat or Compromise?

The exchange of letters between Pope and Emperor on the accession of Leo XIII to the Pontificate heralded the easing of the conflict. In 1880 the Pope, in a letter to the Archbishop of Cologne, recognized the obligation to notify governmental authorities before priests received canonical appointments as pastors. Somewhat later, in answer to a Papal letter, Bismarck used the title Sire in addressing the Pope, a form generally used only in addressing temporal heads of states, which was most pleasing to the Pope. In 1885 Bismarck suggested to Spain that they submit their differences over the Caroline Islands to arbitration by the Pope. Spain wanted the Pope only as mediator, but whether he acted as arbiter or mediator, the Pope was pleased to be called upon, for this was equivalent to tacit recognition of Papal sovereignty. Leo XIII thanked Bismarck and granted him the highest papal order, the Order of Christ. The Lion and the Lamb were bedding down together.

Meanwhile in 1880 Bismarck had begun the long task of modifying the anti-Church laws, and this was continued by further laws in 1882, 1883, 1886; most of these passed over the opposition of the Center party. The Center leaders wanted total repeal of the Falk laws which Bismarck refused. More lenient administration of the laws was undertaken. In 1887 Bismarck was interested in getting a seven-year Army Bill enacted. The Papal secretary requested the Center party to support the measure, but they voted against it and Bismarck dissolved the Reichstag. Again the Papal secretary in somewhat more direct terms urged the Center party to support the military bill and both his notes were published in the electoral campaign. When the Reichstag reassembled the seven-year Army law was passed, with the Center party abstaining. The Center leaders were dejected at what they considered a sell-out to Bismarck, but the Papacy was anxious to bring about a stabilization of the Church in Germany. In payment for aid received, Bismarck in 1887 enacted a final "peace law" and the Pope proclaimed officially that the *Kulturkampf* was at an end. Windthorst was not so easily pacified, and he called attention to *Kulturkampf* legislation that still remained on the statute books.

The separate Catholic Bureau in the Ministry of Culture was not restored; state inspection of schools, civil marriage, the pulpit paragraph, the abolition of the Jesuits, the obligation to announce to governmental authorities appointment of full time clerical appointments all remained. On the other hand the attempt to nationalize the clergy by forcing them into the state system of education had been abandoned; the high secular court for church affairs had been abolished, the power of the church to discipline its clergy restored, religious orders, with the exception of the Jesuits, were again permitted, and there had been some amelioration of the obligation to announce appointment to clerical positions. Above all there was a more lenient enforcement of the laws that still remained on the books.

Different evaluations of the *Kulturkampf* are presented in the following selections. The first is by Bismarck and is taken from his *Reflections and Reminiscences* written well after the close of the struggle. Two selections by German historians follow: the first by Dr. Erich Schmidt-Volkmar, formerly a Chief Counsellor to the German Government, who made use of new archival material as well as a new volume of documents published by the German Democratic Republic (see the bibliography); the second by Georg Franz, Professor at the Marineschule Flensburg-Mürwick, whose interpretive volume relates the Church-State struggle in Germany to the wider European scene. A. J. P. Taylor is an English historian who has written widely on German history; and Adalbert Wahl is the author of a multiple volume history of Imperial Germany.

Afterthoughts

BISMARCK

In the *Kulturkampf*, the parliamentary policy of the government had been crippled by the defection of the Progressive party and its transition to the Centrum. Meantime in the Reichstag, without getting any support from the Conservatives, it was opposed by a majority of Democrats of all shades, bound together by a common enmity, and in league with Poles, Guelfs, friends of France, and Ultramontanes. The consolidation of our new imperial unity was retarded by these circumstances, and would be imperilled were they to continue or to become aggravated. The mischief to the nation might be rendered more serious in this way than by an abandonment of what was in my opinion the superfluous part of the Falk legislation. The indispensable part I held to be the removal of the article from the Constitution, the acquisition of means for combating Polonism, and, above all, the supremacy of the state over the schools. If we carried these points we should still have gained considerably by the *Kulturkampf*, considering the state in which things were before the outbreak of the conflict. I had therefore to come to an agreement with my colleagues concerning the extent to which we might go in our compromise with the Curia. The resistance of the whole body of ministers who had taken part in the conflict was more stubborn than that of my immediate colleagues, and primarily of Falk's successor, in which capacity I had proposed Herr von Puttkamer to the King. But even after this change I could not immediately affect an alteration in the Church policy without causing fresh cabinet troubles unwelcome to the King and undesired by myself. The memories of the days when I sought to gain over fresh partisans are among the most unpleasant of my official career. . . .

Many years of labour were still required before it was possible to enter upon the revision of the May Laws without occasioning fresh troubles in the cabinet, since a majority was wanting for the defence of those laws in parliamentary warfare after the desertion of the Freethought or 'Liberalist' party to the Ultramontane opposition camp. I was satisfied when in opposition to Polonism we succeeded in maintaining as definite gains the relations between school and state imposed by the *Kulturkampf* and the alteration made in the articles of the Constitution relating thereto. Both are, in my opinion, of more value than the injunctions against clerical activity contained in the May Laws and the legal apparatus for catching recalcitrant priests, and I ventured to regard as a considerable gain in itself the abolition of the Catholic section and of the danger to the State arising from its activity in Silesia, Posen, and Prussia. After the Freethought party had not only given up the *Kulturkampf*, prosecuted more by themselves under the leadership of Virchow and his associates than by me, but began to support the Centrum both in parliament and at the elections, the government was in a minority as against the last-named party. In the face of a compact majority consisting of the Centrum, the Progressives, the Social Democrats, the Poles, the Alsatians,

From *Bismarck. The Man and the Statesman, being the Reflections and Reminiscences of Otto Prince von Bismarck. Written and Dictated by Himself after his Retirement from Office*, translated under the supervision of A. J. Butler (2 vols., London: Smith, Elder and Co., 1898), vol. II, pp. 144–149.

and the Guelfs, the policy of Falk had no chance in the Reichstag. For that reason I considered it more politic to pave the way for peace provided the schools remained protected, the Constitution freed from the abolished articles, and the state rid of the Catholic section. . . .

In the year 1886 it was at length possible to terminate the counter-Reformation, partly sought for by me, partly recognised as allowable; and to establish a *modus vivendi* which may still, compared with the *status quo* before 1871, be regarded as a result of the whole *Kulturkampf* favourable to the state.

How permanent this will be, and how long the conflict of denominations will now remain quiet, time alone can show. It depends upon ecclesiastical moods and upon the degree of combativeness, not only of the Pope for the time being and his leading counsellors, but also of the German bishops, and of the more or less High Church tendencies governing the Catholic population at different periods. It is impossible to confine within stated limits the claims of Rome upon countries that have religious equality and a Protestant dynasty. It cannot be done even in purely Catholic states. The conflict that has been waged from time immemorial between priests and kings cannot be brought to a conclusion at the present day, and of all places not in Germany. Before 1870 the condition of things caused the position of the Catholic Church in Prussia itself to be recognised by the Curia as a pattern and more favourable than in most of the purely Catholic countries. In our home politics however, and especially in our parliamentary politics, we could trace no effects of this denominational satisfaction. Long before 1871 the group led by the two Reichenspergers was already permanently attached to the opposition against the government of the Protestant dynasty, though its leaders did not on that account incur the personal stigma of being called disturbers of the peace. In any *modus vivendi* Rome will regard a Protestant dynasty and Church as an irregularity and a disease which it is the duty of its Church to cure. The conviction that this is the case is no reason for the state itself to commence the conflict and to abandon its defensive attitude with regard to the Church of Rome, for all treaties of peace in this world are provisional and only hold good for a time. The political relations between independent powers are the outcome of an unbroken series of events arising either from conflict or from the objection of one or other of the parties to renew the conflict. Any temptation on the part of the Curia to renew the conflict in Germany will always arise from the excitability of the Poles, the desire for power among the nobility, and the superstition of the lower classes fostered by the priests. In the country around Kissingen I have come across German peasants who had had their schooling, and who firmly believed that the priest who stood by the death-bed in the sinful flesh could, by granting or refusing absolution, dispatch the dying man direct to heaven or hell, and that it was therefore necessary to have him for your political friend as well. In Poland I presume it is at least as bad or worse, for the uneducated man is told that German and Lutheran are terms as identical as are Polish and Catholic. Eternal peace with the Roman Curia is in the existing state of affairs as impossible as is peace between France and her neighbours. If human life is nothing but a series of struggles, this is especially so in the mutual relations of independent political bodies, for the adjustment of which no properly constituted court exists with power to enforce its decrees. The Roman Curia, however, is an independent political body, possessing among its unalterable qualities the same propensity to grab all round as is innate in our French neighbours. In its struggles against Protestantism, which no concordat can quiet, it has always the aggressive weapons of proselytism and ambition at its disposal; it tolerates the presence of no other gods.

Compromise

ERICH SCHMIDT-VOLKMAR

EVER since the Peace of Nicias in 421 B.C. during the Peloponnesian War every compromise peace is burdened with the charge of being a "rotten peace." Public opinion values clear-cut stands and decisions in general more highly than an agreement on an equal plane; an unequivocal victory naturally is valued higher than a draw.

And yet there are occasions when the bringing about of a settlement, when the conclusion of a compromise, bears witness to more far-seeing statesmanship than the continuation of a conflict in which the defeat of the opponent appears impossible, or when even victory would have only the doubtful value of a Pyrrhic victory. That is above all true of disputes involving spiritual matters, disputes which extend over rather long periods, and do not lend themselves to a definitive decision. Bismarck found himself in such a situation at the conclusion of the *Kulturkampf*. Burdened with the awareness of the fundamental and epochal significance of this dispute with the Catholic church, during the long years of the struggle he had become convinced that a definitive conclusion of peace was as unattainable as a clear victory of the state over the church. Both of these great and old organizations showed themselves also in this instance as two God-given equal orders which might accept, to be sure, a shift in the demarcation of their powers, but could not permit or suffer the permanent subordination or indeed destruction of one partner. Because of this realization Bismarck was willing to content himself with the more moderate outcome of a *modus vivendi*, namely a condition which secured the position of the state yet left as few wounds as possible on both sides.

Such wounds, however, were numerous at the conclusion of the conflict, indeed not only in the Center and the Catholic church, but also among the Liberals and other protagonists of the state idea.

It should not be denied that Bismarck himself was partly responsible for false expectations in respect to the conclusion of the *Kulturkampf*. Winged words often have their own fate. Born from the conditions of the moment they soon take on the character of a binding declaration which attaches itself like lead to the heels of the author and hinders him from striding forward to an unencumbered solution. And so it happened to Bismarck with his proud expression about going to Canossa, which he coined as an expression of his confident will to victory at the outbreak of the conflict, which, however, having been elevated by the opposing parties to an emotion-charged slogan was to prove a heavy psychological hindrance to forming an objective view of the peace settlement.

It was therefore no wonder that the Liberals made the reproach that contrary to his earlier promise he had nevertheless undertaken a penitential pilgrimage. Indeed, the liberal *Augsburger Allgemeine Zeitung* as early as 1881, at the time of Bismarck's first steps on the path towards peace, had carried an article with the headline "In Canossa," which stated: "The widespread fear, that the Prussian government after the ten-year *Kulturkampf*

From Erich Schmidt-Volkmar, *Der Kulturkampf in Deutschland 1871–1890* (Göttingen: Musterschmidt-Verlag, 1962), pp. 351–355; 358. (Trans. Ernst and Louise Helmreich.) Reprinted by permission of the author and the publisher.

would beat a weak and disgraceful retreat, begins to materialize; we are not on the way to Canossa, but actually are deep in the forecourt of this interesting castle, into which the Imperial Chancellor's proud words promised the nation would never be led. . . ."

Nothing could be more false than this comparison to Canossa, for every discerning person must be struck by the difference between Emperor Henry IV who, deserted by almost all his nobles, had to make a pilgrimage as a penitent to the Pope in Italy to plead for forgiveness in order to save his crown, and the German Imperial Chancellor, the most honored and influential statesman of his time, representative of the strongest continental power, who negotiated with the Pope in the manner of sovereigns and on an equal basis, a Pope who felt himself flattered to be addressed by him as "Sire," and who had to agree that the discussions should take place either on German soil or through the regular diplomatic representative of Prussia at the Vatican. Certainly Bismarck had made concessions, but the opposing side had done likewise: they had met each other half-way. . . .

But liberalism wanted a complete victory, because it had placed itself in the forefront battle line and had put the struggle on an either-or basis, so that it would have to consider a compromise as a defeat. . . .

What was the picture on the side of the Catholic church? It is true it had wrested a series of concessions from the state, but there was little cause for victorious jubilation. It was still too far removed from the favorable position it had occupied at the start of the conflict. Only with sorrowful hearts had the Prussian bishops bowed under the Caudine Forks with the obligation to notify [the state of clerical appointments].

In the Center opinions were divided.

The right wing . . . approved the developments in spite of many reservations: it had during the last phases even directly or indirectly lent its support; the left wing . . . acquiesced only angrily and reluctantly to an unavoidable bitter lot. Several Center representatives considered laying down their mandates. Especially the veterans of the party felt they had lost the battle. To this group first of all belonged Windthorst. This tireless, unafraid and crafty battler must have had the feeling that he had been ground between the millstones of Bismarck's powerful and strategically superior statesmanship and the Vatican's flexible and, so far as he was concerned, unscrupulous diplomacy. He considered the position taken by the Pope as a stab in the back. The reins of leadership in the struggle had to a great extent slipped from his tired hands; in the long years of conflict he had sacrificed his best powers, and a short time after the ending of the *Kulturkampf*, in 1891, he closed his eyes forever. Even the historian of the Center party Bachem must admit: "The *Kulturkampf* was not exactly ended as Windthorst, and with him by far the greater part of his supporters as well as almost the whole press of the Center party, had wished or hoped."

. . . On the other side, however, it must also not be denied that Bismarck had not been able to reach the goal which he had originally set himself, the destruction of the Center and the nationalization of the Catholic Church. In spite of severe wounds and setbacks the Center had emerged from the conflict strengthened; the Catholic Church had shown itself unconquerable and loyal to Rome. The state had indeed not suffered a defeat, but also it had not carried off a clear-cut victory. The outcome of the *Kulturkampf* was a real and therefore viable compromise: it knew neither conqueror nor conquered.

Defensive Victory for the Church

GEORG FRANZ

BISMARCK had begun and fought the *Kulturkampf* as a statesman, as founder of the German national state in opposition to those rising social forces which could only achieve power over the ruins of the monarchical state which he represented. In reality he never had true allies among the parties in parliament, for the parties were the enemies of the state which he represented. It was immaterial, whether Conservative, Liberal, or Center, the parties were for Bismarck tools that he used for the state. The monarchical Prussian state stood above the parties, it was the God-given order of human society. For Bismarck the *Kulturkampf* had been only a means to protect this state against the threats of the Center party. The National Liberals had fought the *Kulturkampf* out of heartfelt conviction, with the goal of creating a national church under the sovereignty of the national state. The liberal left wanted to do away with the churches entirely and recognize only a secular civilization. The Center had arisen as an antiliberal party, as an opposition party to the Prussian-Evangelical state and the small German Empire which it headed. Liberal and clerical were the great opposing philosophies of the century, the latter as a radical form of conservatism. These were the real fronts of the *Kulturkampf*. Its sires were these two parties. In parliament the one appeared as the government, the other as the opposition party. But they were not these in the sense of the Anglo-Saxon pattern. For the Liberals, as the government party, were not "a part of the government"; they could only support it in parliament. The Center was not an opposition party in the Anglo-Saxon sense, one which at any moment may replace in power the governing party, but it was the opposition party because it was anti-state for confessional, particularist, and democratic reasons. Above both parties stood the state, which used them for its own purposes. That was acceptable to the Liberals, but not to the Center. The *Kulturkampf* was basically directed against this party as far as the state was concerned, and the latter used the Liberals as helpful auxiliaries. Thus the *Kulturkampf* in Prussia throughout bore the titanic characteristic marks of its leading statesman, who wanted to make the new party [Center] subservient to the government, and when this did not succeed, wanted to destroy it. After eight years this attempt had failed; out of the struggle against the party, against the will of the Chancellor, a formidable struggle against the Catholic Church had developed which he had never wanted either in this form or of this intensity. In contrast to the Liberals he had carried on the struggle as a defense against the threat which he feared for his work.

What had Bismarck actually achieved for the state? The results, measured against the situation of 1870, were considerable. The political-church Articles of the Constitution remained abrogated; the separate Catholic bureau in the Ministry of Education [*Kultusministerium*] was not reestablished; obligatory civil marriage, state inspection of schools, the Pulpit Paragraph,

From Georg Franz, *Kulturkampf. Staat und Katholische Kirche in Mitteleuropa von der Säkularisation bis zum Abschluss des Preussischen Kulturkampfes* (Munich: Verlag Georg D. W. Callwey, 1954), pp. 276–280. (Trans. Ernst and Louise Helmreich.) Reprinted by permission of the publisher.

the law against Jesuits, the law on the administration of property of Catholic parishes; the law regulating withdrawal from churches, the law (not cancelled until 1890) on exile; the law dealing with Old Catholics — all remained in effect. In restricted measure the regulations as to the education of the clergy and the law concerning vacated bishoprics remained in effect. The most important gains for the state were "the legal provisions in respect to the obligation of the church to notify the state of permanent appointments to parishes and the right of the State to object to such appointments." But in relation to the tremendous display of power, the mighty legal apparatus and the original goals, the outcome of the *Kulturkampf* was a defensive victory for the church. The results of the Prussian *Kulturkampf*, therefore, corresponded throughout with the general results of those in Central Europe. In fact the new Prussian church law also indicated a silent recognition of cancelled Article 15 of the Prussian constitution: "The Evangelical and Roman-Catholic Church, as well as every other Religious Corporation orders and governs its affairs independently." This provision was again included in the Weimar Constitution in Article 137.

Soderini [in his volume on Leo XIII and the German *Kulturkampf*] thus summarizes opinion from the clerical point of view: "the *Kulturkampf* ended with a fruitful alliance between church and state, which freely admitted its unjust actions and no longer placed any restrictions on the Catholic church in carrying out its good work. The church on the other hand admonished its sons to be good citizens and to maintain their loyalty to the fatherland and to the ruling house."

The dispute between church and state had ended with the victorious self assertion of the church over against the modern state. In the struggle against the strongest state of the west it had shown itself unconquerable.

What had the Liberals obtained? They had used up their best powers, and in the contest had been definitely shattered. If the state had emerged from the struggle, thanks to the masterful diplomacy of Bismarck, with an honorable compromise, the *Kulturkampf* had brought a disastrous defeat to liberalism, for the political victor was the Center. In the struggle for the rights of the church it had definitely established itself as a power factor in party politics. Through the Center the fundamental principles of parliamentary democracy had won a decisive victory over the religiously neutral sovereign state. And the Center had smoothed the way for the rising power of socialism. The Social Democratic party had arisen in the shadow of the *Kulturkampf*. State authority had been shattered at least as much by the destructive struggle with the church as by the capitalistic economic system of liberalism. The chief beneficiary of this undermining of state authority, however, was the Socialist movement.

The conclusion of the Prussian *Kulturkampf* was one of the last great accomplishments of the classical diplomacy of the west, whose goal was always to reach a compromise *rebus sic stantibus* between opponents who respected each other as partners to an agreement. Once more the two competing powers concluded a peace that rested on unqualified respect for the existence and autonomy of the partner. Respect for an opponent had been one of the greatest moral achievements of the European state system. But this was placed in question as the *Kulturkampf* clearly demonstrated, by the new rising power of the secular mass parties. The Liberals wished — in the National Liberal Party — the subjection of the church to the state as a national church; the Progressives wanted to see the church put aside altogether; the Center sought a "total capitulation" of the state as well as of its leader. This lack of moderation in establishing their goals is the dark, threatening omen of a new age.

Not least, it is the human greatness of the two antagonists which gives to the great dispute the character of a world wide historical drama. Nature and history appear to have united their strength in unusual fashion when they set the Pope and the Chancellor over against each other. After years of struggle the supreme head of the Catholic Church and the Protestant statesman found themselves allies in the struggle for the great common goal: the maintenance of the existing order through a lasting peace between the two institutions which they represented, state and church.

Bismarck's self-conquest, his broad-minded admission of his mistakes and his firm determination to use his incomparable ability to correct them deserve admiration, as do the wisdom, the forbearance, the perseverance and firmness of Leo XIII, who preferred an honorable compromise to a dangerous attempt to achieve a "total" victory or a fanatical continuation of the struggle, and who unreservedly expressed his respect and esteem to his great opponent.

Political Horse Trading

A. J. P. TAYLOR

Bismarck's jugglery with the Reichstag in the eighteen-eighties rested on a simple calculation. The Conservatives supported him firmly once they were won over by agrarian protection; but he needed further votes to secure a majority. The National Liberals supported the *Kulturkampf*, but opposed protective tariffs and authoritarian government; the Centre opposed the *Kulturkampf*, but supported protective tariffs and perhaps would not mind authoritarian government if it were not applied against themselves. In 1879 Bismarck thought that he had outmanoeuvred the Centre by promoting tariffs, without relaxing the *Kulturkampf*. The manoeuvre did not work: the Centre went back to opposition as soon as the tariffs were passed. In 1880 he had a further, graver disappointment. Leo XIII was anxious to compromise. He disliked the head-on conflict with the modern state and in any case regarded the German Reich as the least of his enemies; if he could settle with Germany, he could play her against France or against his most dangerous op-

ponent, national Italy. In February 1880 Leo XIII, not Bismarck, went to Canossa. He accepted Bismarck's principle that the age-long conflict could not be fought out: church and state should find a workable compromise. As a first gesture he agreed that Roman priests should henceforth register with the state authorities; in return the May-laws would be more laxly applied. Bismarck and Leo XIII had reckoned without the Centre leaders. They refused to settle for anything less than repeal of the May-laws. Windthorst exclaimed: 'Shot in the field! shot in the back!' He thought at first of retiring from politics; then decided, despite Leo XIII's prompting, to oppose all Bismarck's measures. . . . [See "Key Documents, Jacobini letters," *above*]

The army-law passed the new Reichstag for its full seven-year term by an overwhelming majority — 223 to 40. Bismarck enjoyed his triumph in silence and did not go near the tribune. Seven members of the Centre obeyed the pope's instructions and voted for the law; the other eighty-three, including Windthorst, ab-

From A. J. P. Taylor, *Bismarck. The Man and the Statesman* (New York: Alfred A. Knopf, 1955), pp. 201, 224. Reprinted by permission of the publisher.

stained. Leo XIII got his reward. Most of the May-laws were repealed in March 1887, Bismarck personally inspecting the vote in the Prussian diet to ensure that it went the right way. The religious orders were allowed to return, the Roman church recovered control of its seminaries. Bismarck said airily: 'What do I care whether the appointment of a Catholic priest is notified to the state or not — Germany must be at one!' Once he had used the argument of national unity to justify the *Kulturkampf*; now he used the same argument to justify its end.

No Canossa

ADALBERT WAHL

THE question for the retrospective observer is, whether the assertion of Bismarck's "Journey to Canossa" is correct — Canossa, of course, understood in the old fashioned way as a triumph of the Papacy which it of course in truth never was. If all yielding and every change of course is to be considered as Canossa, then there could be no question that Bismarck had gone to Canossa. But it would be well to discontinue this way of speaking in view of the fact that the *Kulturkampf* was substantially ended through unilateral enactment of laws by the state. To drag in the picture of Canossa is also confusing inasmuch as it is likely to cast a shadow on a very great service of Bismarck: the magnificent decision to turn back when he had got on the wrong track, and not as a "theoretical fool" — so he himself said once — continue to hold to a policy for consistency's sake even after the situation had entirely changed since the inauguration of that policy. . . .

But no one will seriously want to maintain that the moderate gains which the state retained from the *Kulturkampf* were a sufficient compensation for the harm that it had brought; among other things the great deepening of the rift, already existing to be sure, which cut through the German nation; the disaffection of countless Catholics from the state; the great strengthening of a party that at that time was still far from being dependable in matters vital to the state; the damage to the Evangelical Church.

To heal the rift and thereby reconcile the Catholic populace with the Evangelical state, that was without doubt, alongside the necessity of the state to alleviate the suffering which its policy had caused countless of its subjects, the highest positive aim in the conclusion of the *Kulturkampf*. In addition, as has often been pointed out earlier, it also had its party-political aspects: the Center on which Prussia and the Empire had now become dependent after it had become so strong and unshakable mainly through the *Kulturkampf*, was now to be won for positive politics on more than an occasional basis. The ending of the *Kulturkampf* has since achieved this purpose to a great extent.

From Adalbert Wahl, *Deutsche Geschichte von der Reichsgründung bis zum Ausbruch des Weltkrieges* (1871 bis 1914) (4 vols., Stuttgart: Verlag W. Kohlhammer, 1926–1936) vol. II, pp. 228; 255–256. (Trans. Ernst and Louise Helmreich). Reprinted by permission of the publisher.

IV. CONFLICT AND SEPARATION: CHURCH AND STATE IN REPUBLICAN FRANCE

Anti-Clericalism and the Third Republic

C. S. PHILLIPS

Ever since the French Revolution anti-clericalism had been an issue in French political life. A notable group of French liberal Catholics, among them Lammenais, Lacordaire, and Montalembert had tried to bring about a reconciliation of the church with current political and scientific thought, but their efforts came to be frowned on by the state and even more by the hierarchy. The church threw its support to the conservative forces during the Second Empire. Bitter church-state conflict characterized the Commune and the founding years of the Third Republic. The following selection by C. S. Phillips of Cambridge University analyzes the anti-clericalism which was a dominant factor in the political life of the republic.

THE triumph of the Republicans in the elections of 1876 was of ill omen for the Church. . . . The only way in which the Church could conceivably have saved itself was to "agree with its adversary quickly" by a frank acceptance of the Republic as the form of government to which France was more and more pledging her adhesion. But such a *ralliement* was not to be thought of at this stage. The clergy still clung to the old alliance between the Altar and the Throne; and for years to come were to be totally incapable of even imagining that any other means of safeguarding the interests of religion was possible. For them the incompatibility between the Church and the Revolution was fundamental and axiomatic. No compromise between them was to be thought of.

The great majority of the influential Catholic laity, wedded as they were to the Royalist cause, shared the same attitude.

The eminent Dominican preacher, Père Didon, discovered this to his cost. When in a Lenten course of sermons preached in 1880 at the fashionable church of La Trinité in Paris, he dared to urge a reconciliation between the Church and modern society, a section of his audience denounced him to the Superior General of his Order, a narrowly intransigent Spaniard. Didon was sentenced to silence and solitude in the Corsican convent of Corbara for eighteen months, and even when he emerged was only allowed to address occasionally a small community of nuns in Paris. He consoled himself by writing his well known *Life of Christ*. It was not till 1892, when the *ralliement* of Catholics to the Republic was well on its way to becoming an accomplished fact, that he was once more allowed full freedom to exercise his ministry. . . .

If the bulk of Catholics thus believed

From C. S. Phillips, *The Church in France, 1848–1907* (London, The Society for Promoting Christian Knowledge, 1936), pp. 184–190. Reprinted with permission of the publisher.

the Church and the Republic to be incompatible, the most active and influential section of the Republican party was of the same opinion. It shared Proudhon's view: "Christian or Republican — there is the dilemma." A striking feature of the years following 1870 is the great development of Freemasonry — a movement which in continental countries (as is well known) is bitterly and militantly antagonistic to revealed religion, and is, in fact, the chief focus of opposition to the Catholic Church. The membership of the various Masonic lodges rapidly increased, and soon included all the leading figures in the Republican party, from Gambetta and Jules Ferry downwards. Side by side with this went a wide and formidable development of their propaganda. For them the one great obstacle in the way of the triumph of the Revolution was the Catholic Church, the influence of which must therefore be brought to an end by a wholesale and uncompromising destruction of the faith of the masses. Of the ways of bringing this about the most efficacious, it was believed, was education. Hence the three-fold Masonic programme — *l'obligation, la gratuité, la laicité*. Education must be compulsory for all, must be without charge and, above all, must be entirely divorced from the teachings of religion. With the object of realizing this programme the *Ligue de l'Enseignement* was brought into existence, in close connection with the Masonic organization. Its founder was Jean Macé, an ardent Freemason and fanatically anti-religious. The doctrines of Freemasonry found firm support in the Radical press, but its most powerful weapon of offence after 1870 was in the multitude of small manuals and *brochures* which were disseminated all over France. The aim of the Masonic cult was quite frankly not merely to destroy Catholicism but to put itself in its place as a kind of "anti-Church." Freemasonry was to become "the Church of the Revolution," with humanity set up as the object of worship in the place of God.

It is worth while to inquire why it was that such doctrines advanced so rapidly in France at this period. To a large extent, of course, they were no new phenomenon. The animus against the Church which found such violent expression during the first French Revolution had never died out. The ideas of Voltaire and Rousseau had commanded a considerable following all through the nineteenth century. It is true that under Napoleon and in the period of the Restoration their expression had been more or less kept in check by the civil authority: and the same policy obtained in the earlier part of the Second Empire. But they lived on, and supplied an important focus of opposition to all three regimes. Moreover, they had entrenched themselves to a considerable extent within the State education system. Such famous professors of the Université as Michelet and Quinet ranked among the most formidable enemies of the Christian religion: and their influence among the younger generation was great. The extensive vogue of the Positivism of Auguste Comte operated in the same direction.

But from about 1860 onwards the activity of so-called "free thought" betrays a new intensity and aggressiveness — an activity now rather favoured than discouraged by the Government for its own purposes. The causes of this were not confined to France but were common to Western Europe generally. The development of historical criticism on the one hand, and of natural science on the other, was battering breaches in the traditional doctrine of Christendom in all its parts: and the enemies of Christianity laid eager hold on the weapons thus placed in their hands. In this connection the work of Ernest Renan is specially notable — a work the influence of which extended beyond France throughout the civilized world. His famous *Vie de Jésus* has been already mentioned in these pages, and was to be followed up by a series of further works on *The Origins of Christianity* that seemed to be inspired by the principle hurled by John Morley in England at the orthodox believers of his time: "We will not refute you: we will explain you." The charm of Renan's style and the mocking keenness of his wit powerfully reinforced the learning and critical acumen displayed in his writings.

The Catholic world was scandalized by them, but unfortunately was content to answer them by abuse rather than by argument. No real attempt was made to meet the challenge of the new knowledge, still less to effect a synthesis between it and the historic faith of the Church. [Bishop] Dupanloup might resign his seat on the Academy as a protest against the election of [the positivist philosopher] Littré: but the more effective protest of a reasoned refutation of the Positivist position was simply beyond his powers. The Catholic apologetic of the period is poor and conventional, even by the admission of Catholics themselves. Père Lecanuet speaks of its "complete sterility" in regard to both philosophy and Bible exegesis — the two fields in which the traditional doctrine was most seriously challenged. And if this weakness marked the learned and instructed, much more was it to be found in the rank and file of the clergy. The training given in the seminaries may often have been thorough enough on the devotional and pastoral side: but on the intellectual side it was sadly to seek. The teaching was poor and uninspiring, the *professeurs* were ill-equipped, the textbooks used in them dull, dry and altogether out of date. Nor did the bishops show any zeal or even interest in their improvement, or desire to encourage the higher studies of their clergy. In consequence the priests turned out by them were for the most part entirely out of touch with the currents of ideas that agitated the more thoughtful and educated members of their flocks. . . .

However it may have been with his wife and daughters, the attitude of the ordinary Frenchman towards his religion was decidedly perfunctory. The church was part of the established order and must normally be treated with respect. But his interest did not in most cases extend to much church-going. M. Isoard, later Bishop of Anneçy, in a book on "Preaching" published in 1870, makes it clear that even at that period men were almost entirely absent from the congregations in the churches. He makes it no less clear that those who did go received little to help them from the sermons they heard. It is not surprising that Catholics so lukewarm and so ill-instructed should have fallen an easy prey to the propaganda of the enemies of religion. Among the many directions in which the growing religious indifference manifested itself was in a notable decline in the number of ecclesiastical vocations. . . . The aristocratic and wealthy classes had for a long time ceased to give their sons to the Church: but now even the ordinary source of recruitment — the lower-middle and working classes, especially in the country — seemed to be drying up.

Nor did the press do anything to supply the defence of religion that was not forthcoming from the pulpit. The most widely read French newspapers were for the most part anti-religious in a greater or less degree, or at least anticlerical. Compared with their circulation, that of a Catholic journal like the *Univers* was negligible. . . .

Chief, however, among the causes that led to the triumph of the Republican anti-clericals over the Church was the identification of the latter with the interests of political and ecclesiastical reaction, its blind opposition to the "principles of 1789" and the liberties of the modern world. Whatever the faults and excesses of the French Revolution may have been, the average Frenchman was convinced that its general results had been wholly beneficial, and had no intention of letting its achievements be swept away in favour of any kind of restoration of the *ancien régime*. It was not monarchy that he disliked so much as the whole cycle of ideas with which in his mind monarchy had come to be associated — the ideas of the Syllabus, in a word. And he knew that with the eclipse of Liberal Catholicism those ideas were more than ever dominant in the Church. Thus it was not difficult for the Republicans to convince him that only through Republicanism, and that eviction of the Church from all influence in politics which was the avowed Republican policy, could the harvest of the Revolution be made secure for future generations. Gambetta showed a sound instinct when he separated the interests of the clerical order from those of religion and coined (or rather borrowed)

his famous battle-cry, *"Le cléricalisme, voilà l'ennemi!"* [Clericalism, there is the enemy!]. Let the clergy confine themselves to their spiritual functions and they would not be molested, at least for the time being. It is the attitude thus fostered, more than any hostility to religion itself, that explains the favour — or at least the acquiescence — with which the nation as a whole was to receive the various measures that were soon to be directed against the Church.

From Laic Laws to Separation

ADRIEN DANSETTE

The conflict between church and state was chiefly centered on the control of education and on the influence of religious orders. Yet it was also a factor influencing most foreign and domestic issues and notably came to the fore in the famous Boulanger and Dreyfus crises. To study the religious conflict in France is to study the history of the Third Republic. The following account of anti-clericalist legislation is by a French scholar Adrien Dansette, Doctor of Law and Chevalier de Legion d'Honneur, who has written, along with other studies, a brilliant two-volume religious history of contemporary France.

THE two main features of the republicans' preparatory programme were educational reform and the dissolution of the religious orders.

An axiom they had inherited from the Revolution laid it down that the foundation of democracy was popular education. "After peace," declared Danton, "education is the first need of the people." As early as 1850, Edgar Quinet had outlined a number of educational reforms, later to be adopted by the Third Republic. From the time of the defeat in the Franco-Prussian war (1870-1), science was venerated as the beginning and end of all human activity and this led the republicans to give the credit for the German victory to the

Prussian schoolmaster, and to discover in their own patriotism further grounds for urging an extensive reorganization of the French educational system. "We regard the written word as a fundamental and irresistible instrument for the promotion of intellectual freedom," said Ferry, in 1880. But what was meant by granting intellectual freedom? Paul Bert, the silver-tongued spokesman of anti-religion, gave a clear indication when he defined primary education as "the whole range of knowledge in the field of positive science but excluding all religious theories and instruction in religious dogma."

The religious orders played such a part in education that it was impossible to make

From Adrien Dansette, *Religious History of Modern France* translated by John Dingle (New York: Herder and Herder, Inc., 1962), vol. II, pp. 35–247. Abridged and reprinted by permission of the publisher.

a radical change in the system without coming into conflict with them, but this was not the only reason why their adversaries were anxious to check their encroachments. By their constitutions, the great religious orders were, more often than not, under the direct authority of the Roman curia, and most of them were the tireless agents of papal policy, a role that some were already playing under the old régime. . . .

The application of the religious policy of the republican party produced a confusing abundance of laws, intended to break down in time the influence of the Church over French life and to prepare for the repudiation, in the more or less distant future, of the concordat. The most important of these laws, passed between the time when the secular republicans secured unchallenged authority in 1879 and the beginning of the Boulangist crisis in 1887, were devoted to educational reform. They were destined seriously to affect the religious orders.

The great architect of this educational reform was Jules Ferry. . . . On 15th March, 1879, he introduced two proposals for a partial reform of education. The first related to the choice of examiners dealing with candidates for degrees from the independent universities. The draft of this bill contained one provision, Article 7, which was completely irrelevant to the issue. The general effect of this article was to exclude from the post of director of any educational institution, public or private, all those who belonged to religious orders that had not been authorized. As we have already mentioned, the State made a distinction between authorized congregations, which alone had the right to hold property, and the non-authorized ones, which were merely tolerated. Only five of the religious orders for men had the necessary legislative sanction. They were the Brothers of the Christian Schools, the Lazarists, the Sulpicians, the Foreign Missions, and the Holy Ghost Fathers. Almost all the rest, and particularly the Dominicans, the Jes-

uits, and the Marists, would consequently no longer be able to teach in either State or private schools and Article 7 would destroy the freedom to teach of a whole category of priests. . . .

When the measure was finally passed [in the Chamber] by a large majority, on 9th July, 1879, the Catholic reaction was unbridled. A general committee to petition for freedom in education was founded and this led to the organization of a counter-petition by the masonic League for Education. . . .

When Article 7 was discussed in the Senate in January, 1880, Freycinet had already taken over the premiership. . . . [He] kept Ferry at the Ministry of Education only because a majority in the Chamber of Deputies would not have tolerated dropping his proposed measure. Freycinet himself was embarrassed and gave no more than lip service to Article 7, which he described as "necessary." Hardly had the Senate rejected this article, than the Chamber of Deputies took its revenge with a motion calling for the application of the laws relating to non-authorized religious orders. The government complied and on 29th March, 1880, published two decrees which came to be known as *the decrees*, a label which they were to retain for more than thirty years. According to these enactments, the unauthorized religious order "known as the order of Jesus" must dissolve itself, and quit the premises it occupied within three months. All other non-authorized orders were required to apply for authorization within the same period, failure to do so entailing their dissolution. Eight or nine thousand men and 100,000 nuns were affected. . . .

The date of the decrees was 29th March. At 8:45 on the morning of 29th June, three months later to the very day, a superintendent of police went to the house of the Jesuits in the Rue de Sèvres in Paris, and, ignoring protests, sealed the door of the chapel in which the Blessed Sacrament was exposed. The next day, the locks of the priests' rooms were picked and their occupants turned out. The Prefect of Police, Andrieux, who had come from a social function, took charge, still wearing his light grey evening gloves. The fathers, surrounded by Catholic parliamentary deputies, left the house and blessed the kneeling crowd. Similar scenes were enacted wherever expulsions took place. The Jesuits applied in vain to the courts, and, equally without effect, a majority of the courts declared themselves competent. The administrative tribunals to which the government referred reversed the verdicts and the expulsions were carried out with nothing more than a delay. . . .

Freycinet, the Prime Minister, unlike Ferry, was not a bitter and energetic secularist. . . . With the question of the Jesuits out of the way, nobody was more willing than he to come to an arrangement over the orders. . . . He agreed to a straight abandonment of insistence on authorization, in return for a declaration renouncing political hostility. . . . Secrecy was preserved and this contributed to the success of the negotiations. Freycinet had not even told his colleagues and the bishops and members of the orders were recommended to be discreet. Signatures to the declaration had only just begun to flow in when on the 30th August the legitimist paper *La Guyenne* . . . published the complete text of the declaration. Both on the left and the extreme right, the press erupted. Freycinet was denounced as a traitor . . . [and] he resigned on 19th September. . . .

Ferry himself formed the new government and the moment for the application of the decrees drew nearer. Both sides made their preparations with dramatic flourishes which seem amusing today, but judgement on such matters is closely bound up with the prevailing circumstances and, at the time, the serio-comic character of the incidents was not appreciated. The members of the religious orders might have been preparing for a siege. They barricaded themselves in their houses, fixed bolts, chains and iron protecting pieces to the doors, and posted sentries to watch for the arrival of the enemy. The government, afraid of unfortunate incidents, decided to carry out the expulsions bit by bit and made its plans in secret. The Carmelites and the Barnabites were the first to be attacked, at the end of October. On 4th November, all the Paris superintendents of police were called to a meeting at Andrieux's headquarters. "Since the December *coup d'État*," wrote the Prefect afterwards, "there had never been any precautionary measures as extensive as these." Eleven religious houses were dealt with at the same time with the aid of an impressive collection of house breaking tools and weapons for boarding operations, such as jimmies, hammers, and axes. . . .

The government, which was particularly anxious to deal with the teaching orders, did not make use of all the powers given to it by the decrees. Nuns were spared everywhere; in Algeria, all the men's congregations were spared, and, in France, some escaped the full rigour of the decrees. Altogether, government representatives forced their way into 261 religious houses, expelling 5,643 members of the orders, but they did not sell up the property of the dissolved congregations. The decrees were applied with the greatest severity against the Jesuits. Their colleges had all been handed over to secular priests or laymen, and if so much as a single member of the order was found to be still employed in one of them, the place was shut on the ground that there had been an attempt to reconstitute an unauthorized congregation.

Ferry must not be regarded as either a Fouché or a Hitler. The expelled members of the religious orders were neither guillotined nor sent to concentration camps, but they were nevertheless victims of a persecution which their political errors might explain but could not justify. After the first flush of victory, the opportunists or moderate republicans began to recognize this and often felt a consequent sense of guilt. When they themselves were in power in the years that followed, they closed their eyes while members of the religious orders slipped back and reoccupied their old houses. Thus, the decrees were ineffectual because they were not applied even by their authors. But they still proved a barrier to the formation of a moderate republic, because they exacerbated the religious conflict to the advantage of extremists on the right and the left.

However violent the conflict of passions may have been at the time, the struggle with the religious orders does not seem in retrospect to have been more than a carelessly provoked incident in the much more serious struggle, which was to determine the character of public education. Four or five years after the decrees, a large number of the expelled orders had resumed a normal life whereas, sixty years from its adoption, Jules Ferry's educational legislation still regulated French elementary education. . . . He introduced into the Chamber a number of measures of which two were particularly important.

One provided for free elementary education and Jules Ferry made this his starting point because compulsion was dependent upon it since an obligation imposing financial sacrifice on parents would have been difficult to impose. Replying to his proposals, Monsignor Freppel contended, in effect, that from the point of view of Catholics, free education was a snare, since, as tax-payers, they would have to provide for schools to which they would not send their children. This argument was not calculated to impress the members of the parliamentary majority whose main concern was to put Church schools at a disadvantage. The law, which was passed through the Chamber fairly easily, was promulgated on 16th June, 1881.

The second of the measures proposed by Jules Ferry related to compulsory schooling. Pressed by the commission, which was in a greater hurry or else bolder than he was, he added the provisions for secularization that he had intended to make the subject of a third measure. Compulsory education, which was to be between the ages of six and thirteen, was based on a right of the child to education which the State claimed the duty of ensuring, even against the misplaced opposition of parents. Catholics were as visibly embarrassed in this debate as they had been in that concerning free education. Behind their arguments could always be discerned their concern about the competition between State schools and the independent schools.

The debate over secularization covered a wider range. The bill proposed to replace "the moral and religious instruction" in the schools by "moral and civil instruction." "The secularization of our national institutions must naturally imply in the end secularization of State education," declared Ferry, adding that it would be against liberty of conscience if children were educated by masters teaching religious doctrines other than those of their parents. The school must therefore take no account of positive religions, but, while it was neutral from the religious point of view, it was not expected to preserve neutrality in the philosophical field. Elementary education was to take no account of Catholicism but was to have a theistic background. The reason for this, Ferry continued, was that the great majority of the teaching profession held theistic views and did so because the majority of the French population also held them. The teacher was thus to inculcate "the good and traditional morality of our forefathers."

The right-wing parties replied that if the instruction given was to be in conformity with the wishes of the majority of the population, it must be Catholic and that it was sufficient to grant to the minority the right to withdraw their children from religious instruction. The neutrality the Minister pretended to establish was illusory. Not to mention God was to deny his existence. The State school would therefore be an atheistic school, quite unacceptable to the Christian conscience.

Jules Ferry was willing to allow the parish priests to give religious instruction within the school buildings, but the Catholic deputies joined with those of the extreme left in rejecting this concession. They wanted to keep everything. In consequence they lost all, or nearly all, for, while the law abolished official religious instruction, it provided for one free day a week when parents could arrange for it to be given to their children if they wished.

The Chamber of Deputies had banished God from the school. In the Senate, Jules Simon tried to put God back. A kind of high priest of natural religion, he gained the support of a certain number of those with theistic views for an amendment according to which "the masters will teach their pupils their duty towards God and towards the fatherland." The amendment was accepted by the Senate but, on 25th July, 1881, the Chamber of Deputies voted to restore the original text.

It was left to the electors to decide between the two. In August and September, 1882, confirming the electoral decisions of 1876 and 1877, they sent back an increased republican majority to the Palais Bourbon. The re-election of a third of the Senate, in January, 1882, enabled the republicans to strengthen their position, and this time Jules Simon's amendment was rejected by both houses, and the law establishing compulsory education and secularization of the schools was promulgated on 29th March, 1882. . . .

For its part, the government was wise enough to avoid the error it had committed in 1879 and 1880, with Article 7 and the decrees. It avoided provoking Catholic opposition by useless irritations. Indeed, deliberately refraining from using the full powers conferred on him by law, the Minister of Education left in the school syllabuses the provision for instruction on the child's duty towards God, and this was not removed until 1941.

In spite of its initially bitter character, the conflict that arose over the school text books provides evidence of the same desire on the part of the government not to re-open recent wounds. To replace the cate-chism, a number of text books were produced, intended to give moral and civic instruction. Four of these were put on the Index in January, 1883. The bishops published the decree of the Holy Office, to which in some cases they themselves added penalties. The Bishop of Annecy, for instance, refused the sacraments to teachers, parents, and children, who failed to destroy the condemned books. Parish priests in Tarn made bonfires of them. The Director of the Ministry retorted by forbidding priests to read the decree of the Index from the pulpit and by suspending the salaries of five bishops and 2,000 parish priests who had failed to comply with his instructions. Once the government had thus indicated that it did not intend to be flouted, peace quickly returned. In November, 1883, Jules Ferry, who had once more become Minister of Education, advised teachers not to insist on the use of the condemned books.

But while religious instruction no longer had any legal place in elementary education, it could hardly be said to have disappeared completely when 3,400 Brothers of the Christian Schools and 15,000 nuns were in charge of State schools. It was not to be expected that these men and women whose lives were devoted to religion would refrain in future from referring to it. Secularization of education could not be complete without secularization of the teaching profession. Already, before the passing of the laws on free, compulsory and secular education, a measure passed on 16th June, 1881, had abolished the declaration of obedience to the bishop, which had hitherto been recognized as a substitute for a certificate of competence in the case of teachers belonging to the religious congregations. Henceforth the certificate of competence was made compulsory for all teachers, except those who had reached the age of thirty-five and had already been teaching for five years. This law, however, failed to produce the effect intended because most of those concerned succeeded in passing the examination and obtaining their certificates. A bill introduced by Paul Bert in 1882 settled the question by removing members of the religious congregations from elementary education, on the ground that they could not be expected to give civic instruction founded on principles incompatible with their own, and that their vows of obedience would lead them to oppose the law each time it seemed in conflict with the orders of their own superiors. Catholics argued in vain that it was contrary to republican principles to exclude a whole category of citizens from public office. After a long debate, Paul Bert's bill became the law of 30th October, 1886, which provided for the replacement of male teachers from the religious orders within five years and that of women as vacancies arose. It also deprived priests of their membership of the schools committees already referred to. Thus the secularization of elementary education became complete.

At least, this was the case as far as the will of the legislature was concerned, but how far did the secularization apply in practice? Catholic influence had too long a tradition and was too strongly anchored in the system built up under the Guizot and Falloux laws to be easily eradicated. Beliefs cannot be made to order and cannot be changed in the twinkling of an eye. Rather, therefore, than attack the old beliefs frontally, at the risk of arousing the opposition of the faithful, was it not better to wean the children from them, without at the same time worrying their parents? The policy adopted was to avoid saying or writing anything that recalled the existence of religious beliefs.

Such a negative policy, however, was not sufficient in itself. It aimed at eliminating religious beliefs but not at replacing them, and the only really successful form of elimination is one accompanied by a replacement. The leaders of the republican movement claimed to be regenerating a France whose military defeat they attributed to the enfeebling effect of religious doctrines. Naturally enough, they turned

to the cult of the fatherland. "We can have no conception," said Jules Ferry, "of the feasts there could be in a religion which has no backsliders, the religion of the fatherland." . . .

But important though these educational laws were, they should not tempt us to overlook other legislative efforts, equally designed to establish a secular society.

In the administrative and official fields, for instance, a number of measures call for consideration. Soldiers rendering military honours were ordered to remain outside the churches. The army was forbidden to escort religious processions and to provide sentries to guard episcopal palaces. Public prayers were forbidden. Control of public order within churches was vested in the local mayor, who had the right to have the bells rung for purely civil ceremonies. Moreover, being responsible for order on the public highway, the mayor was able to forbid religious processions.

In the social sphere, compulsory Sunday rest was regarded as a sign of clericalism and was abolished. It was not reestablished until a quarter of a century later, when it was deemed necessary to prevent the exploitation of labour. Cafés, taverns, and wine shops, traditional centres of the antireligious movement, ceased to need administrative authorization. It was forbidden to bury people in different parts of cemeteries according to their religious beliefs or the circumstances of their deaths. This meant that cemeteries could no longer have separate sections set apart for those professing different religions, or for suicides. The office of military chaplain was abolished. The formula "no exemption for priests" was applied and Church students were obliged to spend a year with the colours (ordinary military service lasted three years). In the event of mobilization, it was intended that clerics should do ambulance work, or serve in the medical corps. This last measure, which was the first step towards putting clergy and lay folk on the same footing with regard to military service, merits particular attention. The republican majority voted for it, not in order to gain 1,500 more conscripts a year, but to reduce the number of would-be priests, previously increased by this traditional exemption. In practice, however, this withdrawal of their special privilege caused a drop in the number of clerical students only for a few years, and had the advantage of giving them an experience of life that was particularly useful in their apostolic mission. Finally, by ensuring that the clergy contributed to national defence during the first world war, the measure helped to make less bitter religious conflicts that would have been dangerously exacerbated had the clergy been exempted.

The substitution of lay women for nuns in the hospitals constituted another step in the secularization of social life. At the request of the municipal council of Paris, which alleged that the nuns were badly trained for their work and put pressure on their patients, the government began to eliminate them from the hospitals in the capital. This movement varied in intensity according to the ebb and flow of political influences until 1907, when the secularization of the hospitals was completed under Clemenceau's first cabinet. In the period after 1888, five provincial towns followed the example of the capital.

In 1884, divorce was reinserted into the civil code. The earlier divorce laws had been repealed under the Restoration and the change gave rise to violent arguments. As with the new educational régime, the introduction of divorce was a reform of which the full consequences were to be appreciated only over a long period.

Important positions which Catholics had conquered in the past three-quarters of a century were thus destroyed or shaken within the space of a few years. The forces responsible for this assault were, it is true, the fruit of anti-religious doctrines and feelings, but they would not have been so violently hostile had the Church not shown such undisguised opposition to modern society under the influence of an unyielding pontificate lasting thirty years.

By a tragic coincidence, the beginning of a new pontificate, inspired by an altogether different spirit in which conciliation verged on good will, found modern society unleashing its most implacable offensive against the Church.

WALDECK-ROUSSEAU AND REPUBLICAN DEFENCE
(1899–1902)

Between 1878 and 1879 Leo XIII became Pope and the secular republicans came to power in France. The period thus definitely marked a turning point in the contemporary religious history of France. For most of the following two decades, there was a slow evolution in religious affairs to which it would be quite arbitrary to assign any precise dates. With the end of the century, changes again came rapidly. In 1899, Waldeck-Rousseau launched a new attack on the regular clergy. In 1902, under Combes, this offensive was extended beyond the clergy to Catholicism in general. The following year brought the death of a Pope who had consistently striven for reconciliation between the Church and modern society, and his successor, more concerned with the maintenance of principles, did not hesitate to assert emphatically the rights of the Church, regardless of the results of his intransigence. But Leo XIII had survived for several years a dream that belonged to the past or the future rather than the present. The opening of the new chapter in France's religious history must thus be placed in 1899. . . .

The new Prime Minister [Waldeck-Rousseau] whose father had been among those proscribed at the time of Louis Napoleon's *coup d'État* on 2nd December, 1851, was typical of those described as "moderate republicans but not moderately republican," who felt themselves pushed to the left as a result of the Dreyfus reaction. . . . He was imbued with a high ideal of the importance of public office and the Dreyfus affair seemed to him a judicial scandal, affecting the fundamental principles on which the law rests. He saw the monarchist plot, the nationalist agitation, and the military intrigues as political scandals threatening national sovereignty. The action of the members of the religious orders also threatened the supremacy of the civil society. Anti-clericalism represented for him a necessary way of being consistent and persevering in the public service. . . .

Waldeck-Rousseau did not lack arguments against the religious orders. On more than one occasion, he outlined ideas concerning them that he had already held before becoming Prime Minister. They revealed his own constant preoccupation with the need for a strong State provided with the necessary judicial machinery. The concordat had become a dead letter, he urged, and, although they were, in fact, not strictly necessary to the Church, the religious orders had developed tremendously in numbers, thanks to the tolerance of the clerical governments of the Second Empire and of the National Assembly. They were larger than they had been in 1789 and were freely gathering property held in mortmain. This constituted an immediate instrument of domination and would furnish a war chest for the future. They resisted the tax laws although their fortune in real estate alone had amounted to 700 million francs in 1880 and had passed the milliard mark in 1900. They had descended into the political arena and indulged in electoral propaganda. They were training the youth in a counter-revolutionary spirit, thus breaking the moral unity of the country and preparing for a struggle between two rival sections of society. It was necessary, by eliminating the most dangerous elements composed of the intriguers and business men among the monks, to check the formation of a rival force within the State tending to usurp all authority, and it was also necessary to bring those who remained under close control. . . .

Waldeck-Rousseau wanted to limit the authority of the orders and to bring them

under the yoke of republican law. As early as 14th November, 1899, he submitted a bill relating to associations which aimed at defining the future situation of the religious orders.

Without waiting for it to be passed, the Prime Minister struck at the Assumptionists, whose incursions in the political field had met with almost unanimous opposition. . . . The police went to the offices of the *Bonne Presse;* and Père Bailly, the editor of *La Croix,* and Père Adéodat, chairman of the Justice and Equality Committee, were prosecuted together with some others for an offence against Article 291 of the penal code which made it necessary to obtain government sanction before forming an association of more than twenty people. On 24th January, 1900, the court ordered the dissolution of the Assumptionist Order. Waldeck-Rousseau also reproved Cardinal Richard, who had visited the Assumptionist Fathers to express episcopal sympathy, and suspended the salaries of six bishops who had protested against the sentence of dissolution. . . .

Associations in general were governed by Article 291 of the penal code under which the Assumptionists had been condemned. As for the special type of associations known as religious orders, we have already seen that the relevant legal provisions, the most recent of which went back to the Restoration period, made it necessary for them to obtain special permission. . . .

Waldeck-Rousseau did not intend to do more than submit them to control, but the committee entrusted with the examination of the bill was out to destroy them and for authorization by decree substituted provision for legislative authorization which had to be applied for within three months. The committee added a clause denying the right to teach to anybody who had belonged to a non-authorized religious order. This was the Article 7, previously proposed by Jules Ferry, to which we have already referred. In spite of the opposition of some of the moderates, who agreed with Ribot that "one must be tolerant even towards the intolerant," the bill, altered in this way and accepted by the government, became law on 9th July, 1901, having been passed in the Chamber by 303 votes against 224. . . .

Waldeck-Rousseau had promised the Holy See that the law would be applied in "a most benevolently liberal spirit." The question whether or not to comply was one that affected not only the existence of the religious orders themselves but that of all the enterprises for which they were responsible. Catholics were on the whole violently hostile to Waldeck-Rousseau's policy but they had shed some of their illusions in the past twenty years. Whereas the orders had opposed Ferry's decrees, on this occasion 615 congregations requested authorization. Only 215 refrained from doing so. They included the Jesuits who were "predestined victims."

The Chamber elected in 1898 might or might not have accepted Waldeck-Rousseau's suggestion that most of the authorizations asked for should be granted. Before the question came up for discussion, however, the parliamentary elections of May, 1902, had intervened. . . .

The election campaign centred around the religious question, a factor which once more provoked anti-clerical reactions. As a result of the elections, the existing majority was increased by thirty and was imbued with a more aggressive spirit. The struggle had been bitter and the deputies came back from their constituencies in an angry mood. Waldeck-Rousseau was a man of the centre, but in the previous parliament, instead of acting as a leader, he had allowed himself to be led by the left wing. In the new Chamber, the left was even more numerous and clear-cut in its attitude than before. Disillusioned and already beginning to suffer from the disease that was eventually to prove fatal, Waldeck-Rousseau retired, and, by a strange error of judgment, suggested as his successor a man who was to go so far in betraying his intentions as to take up an exactly opposite position. With Émile Combes, republican

defence was to be transformed into an anti-Catholic offensive.

ÉMILE COMBES AND SECULARISM (1902–1904)

Combes made use of the 1901 law from the time he took office, first as a means of destroying the system of education created by the religious orders and then to destroy the orders themselves. The various stages in this work of destruction were somewhat confused since the legal positions of the various orders and the establishments they had created differed.

More than 2,500 schools, founded before the law of 1901, most of them run by nuns, were regarded as non-authorized establishments, run by authorized orders. Waldeck-Rousseau considered that the 1901 law did not apply to them, but that they came under that of 1886 dealing with elementary education. Relying, therefore, on the Prime Minister's statement, these schools had not attempted to obtain authorization. Combes broke the undertaking given by his predecessor and considered himself justified in shutting them at a week's notice since they had not applied for authorization within the period of grace allowed. . . .

Meanwhile, the government's grip on the religious orders continued to tighten. Eleven thousand hospitals and educational establishments, not in themselves authorized, but owned by authorized religious orders, had asked to be recognized. Combes persuaded the *Conseil d'État* not to press its right to scrutinize the law, refused the authorizations, and proceeded to close the various houses throughout 1903.

There remained the further case of the non-authorized congregations which had duly made application. Waldeck-Rousseau's idea had been to have as many bills as there were applications and the *Conseil d'État* had advised that the question of acceptance or refusal of an authorization should be referred to each of the two Chambers and that, in the meantime, the orders were to be tolerated as before. Combes obtained from the *Conseil d'État* a new ruling to the effect that a refusal by one Chamber alone would be enough to veto an authorization. In order to prevent important cases coming before the Senate, on which he was less able to count, the Prime Minister had fifty-four demands by men's orders transferred to the Chamber of Deputies with the recommendation that they should be rejected. Accepting the advice of the parliamentary committee concerned, he divided them into three groups, each one of which was dealt with in a separate bill. The first group was composed of twenty-five orders described as "teaching," the second of twenty-two, described as "preaching," and the third containing the single order of the Carthusians, designated "commercial." These categories were arbitrary, but the majority had made up its mind. "I am speaking to a Chamber so prejudiced that any debate is more or less impossible," said Ribot. In spite of his efforts, and those of other moderates such as Aynard and Leygues, the demands for authorization were rejected globally in March, 1903.

Three hundred and ninety women's orders had also made application. Combes again brought eighty-one of the cases before the Chamber of Deputies. These concerned the congregations designated teaching orders and the demands were rejected, once more globally, in June. He had the six applications from men's orders in the categories of hospitalers, missionaries, and contemplatives submitted to the Senate, urging in the case of five of them that the requests should be granted. These were the White Fathers, the Lyons Fathers, the Cistercians, the Trappists, and the Brothers Hospitalers of St. John of God. There was no debate in these cases and the orders concerned continued to be tolerated, just as were those orders for both sexes whose applications had not come before parliament. The sixth application came from Don Bosco's Salesians and this was refused in July, on Combes' recommendation. . . .

During the winter and the spring of 1904, further anti-clerical measures were adopted. Decrees were made providing for the removal of the crucifix from court rooms and forbidding soldiers to join professional religious groups. The examination for the degree of *agrégé* [prized university degree giving the right to teach at secondary schools and universities] was closed to all ecclesiastics, in spite of the fact that some young priests had been studying for it for years. Some months later, in December 1904, a law was passed transferring responsibility for burials from the church councils, which had been the competent authorities since 1809, to the municipalities.

These were secondary matters and Combes did not overlook his main aim, which was to exclude the religious orders from the educational field altogether, after having dissolved the non-authorized orders. By October 1903, more than 10,000 schools run by religious orders had already been closed and of these only 6,000 were later reopened, most of them being run by religious who had become secularized. These schools belonged to orders that had not been authorized. The authorized orders, which also had schools, did not come under the law of 1901 but were to be proceeded against under a special law.

Several draft bills and proposals with this aim in view were debated at the end of 1903 and the beginning of 1904. Among the radicals most hostile to religion were some anxious to make the opening of private religious establishments subject to direct parliamentary approval, a system which would in effect have created a monopoly.

Combes was, moreover, not in favour of a State monopoly, but aimed merely at eliminating teaching by members of the religious orders. His approach was simple. Besides the 2,500 scholastic establishments closed during the summer of 1902, the authorized orders also had 8,200 other establishments authorized individually. These two sets of schools should not be treated differently by virtue of permission given fifty or even eighty years previously, maintained Combes. The idea was, as a report by Buisson put it, to establish a legal incompatibility between teaching and monasticism in all its forms, since monasticism implied an abdication of the human personality. A law passed on 7th July, 1904, forbade members of religious orders to teach, whatever the legal situation of their particular order. Their houses were to be shut within ten years. The teaching orders were to be dissolved and liquidated, the only houses to be spared being the noviciates training teaching staffs for French schools abroad, in the colonies, and in the countries under protectorate. Thus, excellent teachers had to give up their classes simply because they were members of the orders. The President of the Republic, who was not in the least sectarian, signed the law very much under protest and Mme. Loubet indignantly cried that they were dishonouring her husband. From 1904 to 1911, 1,843 schools belonging to religious orders were closed and 272 cases were brought in the courts for failure to apply the law. Altogether, these affected 1,429 people, of whom 637 were found guilty.

The property of orders wound up under the laws of 1901 and 1904 could not be shared out among the members of the orders concerned but belonged to the State or was, in other words, confiscated. The value amounted to 500 million francs according to Catholics, and not to a milliard as the administration alleged, but in any case it was necessary to realize the sum. This disastrous liquidation was finally to degenerate into fraud. The religious authorities censured those who bought the properties and the prices realized were sometimes as low as a fifth and even a tenth of the estimated value. By 1906, a sixth of the property had been sold and the proceeds came to thirty-two million francs, of which seventeen millions were swallowed up by expenses and professional fees. Combes adapted Mme. Loubet's words, "They are going to dishonour my work," he said. It was in vain that the Senate appointed a commission. The scandal came to a head in 1910. A liquidator named Duez was arrested for having, among other malpractices, restored their property to the religious orders in return for payment. Duez went to prison but the money was never recovered. . . .

The secular philosophy inspiring Combes' ministry influenced foreign affairs as well as domestic politics. Hardly had the law on teaching by the religious orders been passed than the government put an end to a period of quarrels with the Holy See by breaking off diplomatic relations.

SEPARATION OF CHURCH AND STATE (1905–8)

Nowadays, it is regarded as normal that France should have diplomatic relations with the Holy See and that Church and State should be separate. Diplomatic relations are necessary because, apart from any doctrinal considerations, France must be represented wherever she has interests to defend. The separation is equally necessary because, in a democracy based on the sovereignty of a people divided in their religious beliefs, the State owes the Church only liberty. That at least is the commonly held opinion.

The situation was the exact opposite in 1904. The real reasons for the breaking off of diplomatic relations were ideological and the concordat remained and was to continue in force for a further eighteen months. The continued maintenance of an official form of worship in a State that had become hostile to it and did not recognize its head was clearly paradoxical. Logically, the link between Church and State contracted in 1801 under the consular government should have been broken from 1879 onwards when the secular republicans came to power. The system survived the factors bringing it into being only because of an inertia of which history provides many examples. . . .

Secular radicals regarded separation as an arm which should be wielded as soon as possible in order to render the clergy powerless and uproot Catholicism. "People should realize," wrote Ranc, "that separation has never been for us anything more than a means. Our aim is the complete secularization of the State and an end to the Church's influence." In their innermost hearts many radical deputies may not have wanted separation, but in the future they would have to follow the same line as their comrades, more particularly as they were spurred on by the pressure of socialist example. . . .

Nearly all the bishops, the clergy, and the laity remained in favour of the concordat for a number of doctrinal, historical, and practical reasons. The Church has always urged the union of the two powers and has several times condemned the evil of separation. In practice, separation was associated in French minds with the tragic conditions following the revolutionary upheaval and was linked with the memory of persecutions. Moreover, a breach of the 1801 concordat would deprive the Church of a budget of thirty-five million francs without which it could only with difficulty provide for its priests, the upkeep of buildings, and the continuance of its various enterprises.

The number of opponents of the concordat voting against the religious affairs estimates had grown considerably in the new Chamber and, in 1903, it reached the figure of 237. . . . A committee of twenty-three members was appointed in June, 1903, and it voted in favour of reform by a majority of two votes. It completed its work in July, 1904, producing a text which was fairly liberal, thanks principally to the *rapporteur*, Aristide Briand. Combes declared his own formal acceptance of separation in a speech at Auxerre, on 4th September, and, in the weeks that followed, the assembly of the Grand Orient, the international congress of free thought, the annual congresses of the *Ligue de l'Enseignement*, and the radical party all joined in the chorus. . . .

Combes' bill was never destined to be debated since attention was directed elsewhere. A political scandal had just broken out which endangered the government and was finally to bring it down. . . . On 14th January, 1905, the Prime Minister still managed to obtain a majority of six votes, but he had had to promise secretly before the sitting ended that he would resign, and on 18th January, he decided to go, but accompanied his letter of resignation with a written justification of his policy. Such a thing had never yet been done. Combes alleged that he was going in order to save the policy of separation, which his opponents were ready to sacrifice in order to throw him out. In fact, however, he was forced to go by the defection of the socialists and the moderates. . . .

Combes was concerned only with the religious question. His successor, Rouvier, a financier, turned his attention to more mundane matters and hardly bothered about religion. He did not even take part in the debates on the separation bill, and when someone expressed surprise at his absence, he replied, "I have got my man inside there. He will tell them all they want to know." His "man" was the Minister for Religious Affairs, Bienvenu-Martin. . . . When the debate was about to open in the Chamber, he was saying in the lobbies, "We shall be talking about this question again in ten years' time." He was wrong. The time had come. The fall of the previous government had itself brought matters to a head by ensuring for the separation bill the support of moderates who had previously opposed it because Combes was trying to put it through in a civil war spirit.

Bienvenu-Martin's proposed text lay half-way between that of Combes [proposed November, 1904] and that of the committee, but it was the committee's version that was debated in the Chamber from March to July, 1905. . . .

All the mutual grievances of the Church and the Republic were exchanged during the long debate, lasting three months. . . . The separation bill was finally passed in the Palais Bourbon by 341 votes to 233 and, after going to the Senate at the Luxembourg, it became the law of December, 1905. Today it still governs relations between Church and State. The concordat had described Catholicism as "the religion of the majority of French people." The new law proclaimed that the Republic did not recognize any form of religion, nor did it pay the salaries of its ministers (Article 2). This meant that Calvinism, Catholicism, and Judaism lost their privileges. The Church was, therefore, in future answerable only to the Holy See. The State ceased to give it an official position in the order of precedence and to concern itself with the appointment of the Church's ministers or with their salaries. The ministers themselves ceased to be affected by the duties and prohibitions laid down in the organic articles. Ownership of the churches, chapels, archiepiscopal and episcopal palaces, presbyteries, and seminaries, had been vested in the State, the departments, and the communes since the Revolution, but the buildings concerned had been set aside for religious purposes under the Consulate and the Empire. It was now necessary to decide what to do with these buildings, and with the goods, chattels, and revenues and with other public establishments connected with religion. Organizations for which French law had hitherto made provision, such as societies, associations, and professional bodies, did not have the necessary powers, and the separation law therefore provided for associations of a new type, in conformity with the law of 1901, but slightly modified in order to adapt them to the end in view. Described as religious associations, they were to be set up within a year and to be in harmony with the general provisions regulating religious worship (Article 4). Their membership was to vary according to the size of the commune (Article 19). Should the ownership of property be disputed by a number of these associations, Article 8 stipulated that the case would be argued before the *Conseil d'État,* which would deliver a judgement "taking account of all the circumstances in the case." . . .

To summarize then, the law had its problems as well as its advantages for Catholics. It gave them freedom in many respects. Freedom to meet and freedom to hold national and regional councils, and diocesan synods were recovered. There was also freedom of the pen and the spoken word. From bishops to curates, ecclesiastics could write and say from the pulpit what they wished, without being under the sordid threat of the procedure laid down for dealing with alleged breaches of the concordat, and without risk of their salaries being suspended. The Church was also free to make its own appointments. It was the Holy See and not the government that would in future appoint bishops and the Church could determine ecclesiastical boundaries and build churches and chapels. Under the concordat, new buildings of this kind had to have the consent of the State.

But for this freedom the Church had to pay dearly. The law did not conform either to the doctrinal ideal of the Church or to the wishes of the ecclesiastical authorities, and parliamentarians who had voted for it were excommunicated. Henceforth the State took no account of Catholicism and its clergy were deprived of any official status. Apart from a diminution of prestige, the Church also suffered considerable material loss through the abolition of the religious affairs budget on which it had depended ever since the concordat. The religious associations were the pivots of the Church's organization under the new order. They had to ensure religious worship, together with the funds necessary for doing so, and find the money for the training and upkeep of priests. They created a serious problem. It looked as though with the help of the *Conseil d'État,* the authority of the laymen, who formed a majority on these associations, might be substituted for that of the hierarchy, a procedure that would open the way for attempted schism.

Whatever its defects and dangers, the law had been passed. Henceforth the links between Church and State were broken and it was the State that had broken them. The Church had to decide what to do in these changed circumstances. It could accept the new régime or, alternatively, refuse to form the religious associations. The latter course, however, would have serious consequences because, under the text as passed by parliament, the associations had to be set up within a prescribed period and, if they were not, the Church stood to lose a fortune estimated at 331 million francs and would lose control, not only of bishops' palaces, seminaries, and presbyteries, but even of the churches themselves, which the State would have the right to secularize.

But however great the cost, the Church decided to accept it and condemned the proposed solution of religious associations. Now that the separation has become part of French national life and works without a hitch, this decision may be found surprising. Long years of more peaceful policies and good will on both sides have made it possible to accept without reserve a law whose application has been fixed by custom and by a fresh series of negotiations. At the time it was questionable whether the law really could be accepted and it needed courage for a Catholic to affirm that it could. The Church could not properly assess the benefits it was to derive from the law in the future. Judging it in the light of its principles, its own history, and the attendant circumstances, the Church regarded the law as a disaster. . . .

On 11th February, 1906, the Pope promulgated the encyclical *Vehementer*. This condemned the principle of the separation as the overthrowing of the order "established for the world by God in his wisdom" — an order which necessitated harmony between the religious and the civil society. In spite of the favourable opinion of the French cardinals, the encyclical also condemned the provisions of the law. "The law . . . hands over the administration and guardianship of religious worship not to the hierarchical body divinely instituted by the Saviour, but to an association of lay persons. . . . It must be apparent to all, even at a first glance, that such regulations are offensive to the Church, and that they will infringe its rights and be at variance with its divine constitution."

This, however, was not the final word. . . . [Important amendments to the Separation Law enacted in 1907 and 1908 made the relationship of the church to the religious associations more acceptable to church authorities and did much to restore better feeling between church and state.]

The Church lost a great part of its belongings, but at least gained in freedom from the exchange. The Church was not, however, an isolated little world of its own, able to live without reference to the State, and still had to observe the requirements of a public order that might be upset by the clergy in fulfilling or exceeding their priestly duties. The regulations governing public order could be made so strict as to hamper the Church in its own sphere. The Church needed property to accomplish its mission, but could not own it after having itself abandoned the means of doing so by rejecting the church associations. Such problems of public and private law were arising daily.

The law of 2nd January [1907] had left church buildings at the disposal of the Church and the faithful. But the upkeep and repair of these buildings had to be provided for. When the communal authorities, which owned the buildings, would not provide the funds for their upkeep, it was the parish priest himself who shouldered the responsibility, with the help of contributions from the faithful. Major repairs raised a problem because of their high cost, and they were generally undertaken as far as possible by the communes. In cases where the communes refused, the church structures deteriorated to such an extent that they were sometimes liable to fall into ruins. Barrès was deeply concerned about the matter and between 1910 and 1913 conducted a campaign alternately in the *Écho de Paris* and from the rostrum of the Chamber to remedy "the great distress of the churches of France." He persuaded Briand to agree that those built be-

fore 1800 should be the responsibility of
the Ministry of Fine Arts and that money
contributed by Catholics for the repair of
churches should be specially administered.

Sometimes religious activities provided
a threat to public order, the maintenance
of which was the responsibility of the municipal authorities. Sectarian councils
found an excuse in this for a sordid little
war, with an occasionally lively side, which
remained bitter right up to the first world
war.

Questions relating to the hours of opening and closing of church doors, religious
services, the proper ordering of ceremonies, the posting of bills on church walls,
and exterior decoration provided little difficulty, but the same could not be said of
funerals, religious processions, and bell

ringing. Formally appealed to from all
quarters, the *Conseil d'État* gradually
worked out a system of case law and this
became the basis of customs now accepted
throughout France. For example, it made
a distinction between processions properly
so-called, concerning which the mayor had
the final decision, and traditional ceremonies, such as funeral processions and the
carrying of the Viaticum, which the mayor
was not empowered to prevent. Finally,
taking an even more liberal attitude, the
Conseil d'État restricted the powers of the
mayor to cases where there was a threat to
public order. In the same way, it allowed
restrictions on bell ringing only for reasons
of security or the peace of the neighborhood.

Dechristianization or Religious Revival?

France in contrast to Italy or Germany adopted the radical settlement,
the complete separation of church and state. Just what did this involve? The
following selections evaluate the settlement and furnish some answers to this
question. The first, by Professor Evelyn M. Acomb of State University College (New Paltz, New York), centers on the early laic laws; while the second
by D. W. Brogan, a British historian who has made modern French history his
own special field, concentrates on the final law of separation. Dealing more
directly with the overall results of the conflict are the last three selections. The
first of these is by Georg Franz, German scholar of the *Kulturkampf*; the second by Adrien Dansette, whose admirable account of the course of secularist
legislation is given above; and the third is by Albert Guérard, for many years
professor at Stanford University.

The Laic Laws — State Supremacy

EVELYN M. ACOMB

From the foregoing study it should
be evident that no one factor was
responsible for the enactment of the laic
laws. The position of the Church in 1876
was such as to make ·it vulnerable to at-

tack. Its growing ultramontanism and increasing influence in education, philan-
thropy, the army, and politics during the
years of monarchist coalitions aroused
alarm among the advocates of an all-pow-

From Evelyn M. Acomb, *The French Laic Laws* (1879–1889), (New York: The Columbia University Press, 1941), pp. 249–259 *passim*. Reprinted by permission of the publisher.

erful national state. Republicans coveted the positions held by the secular and regular clergy. The status of the Church under the Concordat and Organic Articles was ill-defined, for, in the course of the nineteenth century, certain provisions of those measures had become dead letters, especially those of a Gallican character. The Church had obtained additional concessions, such as the right of the pope to give prior consent to the appointment of bishops by the government, the exemption of the clergy from military service, and the monopoly of funerals. Some of the terminology of the Concordat was ambiguous and some of its omissions, especially that of any reference to the religious orders, were used by the radicals for their own advantage. Within the Church itself there were signs of weakness. The number of candidates for the priesthood was rapidly falling off, and the clergy was less highly educated than it had been. Catholics offered few constructive proposals for reform and were divided by their political, doctrinal, and social views. The aristocratic outlook of their leaders alienated the working classes.

The sympathy expressed by many members of the Church for the monarchist cause antagonized the republicans, whose position was insecure while the pretenders lived. The foolish attempt of Marshal MacMahon to dismiss a government supported by a majority in the Chamber brought retaliation upon the Church, which was accused of encouraging this move. The promulgation of the *Syllabus of Errors* in 1864 and the Declaration of Papal Infallibility in 1871 seemed to deny the very principles upon which the republic was founded. . . .

The attack upon the Church would not have been so generally supported if the ground had not been prepared by the anticlerical philosophies then popular. Most influential of all were the ideas of Auguste Comte, as revised by his disciple, Littré. The assertion that scientific knowledge alone was valid, that mankind could gradually attain perfection through the intellec-

tual and moral development of the masses, that woman was destined to be the moral guardian of the family, and that the state should be separate from the church contradicted fundamental conceptions of Catholicism and inspired the laic laws. The views of Comte and Littré on education, the position of the priesthood, the significance of the French Revolution, the function of the industrialists and workers, centralized government, and civil liberties also underlay the legislation. . . .

The demand for reform of the French school system, which had been revived during the last years of the Second Empire, encouraged discussion of the relative merits of state and religious schools and facilitated the anti-clerical attack upon Catholic schools. Education in the latter was denounced for its preoccupation with memory work and the classics and neglect of science and "modern" ideas. Members of the religious orders were declared ill-prepared to teach. It was said that instruction would benefit by the creation of a real competition between public and private schools. Although both educational systems were obviously in need of improvement, the private schools were discriminated against in the endeavor to strengthen the schools of the state.

Anti-clericalism was an expedient policy for the opportunists to pursue for several reasons. It was useful as a weapon against the monarchists, who were united in their loyalty to the Church. It also served to retain the allegiance of the radicals, through whose aid Gambetta had risen to power, whose voice was loudly heard in the Chamber, and who were in the majority in the municipal council of Paris. It was substituted for abrogation of the Concordat and social reforms which must be postponed until the conservative *bourgeoisie* and peasantry had been won over to the republic through a peaceful and profitable régime. Since France was still weak from the crushing blow of 1871, Gambetta, although he did not relinquish the hope of revenge, endeavored to remain at peace until the country was re-armed and the republic secure. Anti-clericalism assured peaceful relations with Italy, which feared that France might champion the claims of the Pope to temporal power. It promoted friendship with Germany, which had carried on its own *Kulturkampf* and believed that an anti-clerical, conservative republic in France would be weak at home and abroad. And it was a policy with which England, Austria, and Russia were sympathetic. The republicans cleverly substituted it for *revanche* in political campaigns and contrived to fasten upon the monarchists the stigma of inciting neighboring countries to war. They were abetted by Bismarck, who used his influence to persuade the French electorate that an ultramontane, monarchical régime would endanger the cordial relations between France and Germany.

Republican, Jacobin nationalism contributed to the anti-clerical movement through the propagation of its ideals. The thirst for revenge led to an imitation of Prussian education, military methods, and science. The traditions and principles of the French Revolution filled the minds of the republican statesmen and inspired the legislation which they enacted. Freedom of conscience was used to justify the secularization of the school, the courts, the army, cemeteries, funerals, marriages, and holidays. Equality and fraternity were invoked to defend free, compulsory, and lay primary education and universal military service. Belief in the authority of force, derived from Comte and from the success of Prussian militarism, led to the exaltation of ideals far removed from those of the Christian Church. The national army was to be not only an instrument of defense, but also a source of patriotic inspiration. The more radical republicans even believed that some day faith in the fatherland might replace the supernatural and divisive dogmas of Catholicism.

Republican, Jacobin nationalism was hostile to the Church, whose privileges it regarded as derogatory to the sovereignty of the national state and as inimical to freedom of conscience. To civil society it attributed mankind's achievement of freedom of conscience and thought, and accused the Church of antipathy to free investigation, scientific discoveries, and social reform. It declared that an organization with a foreign head could not be patriotic and that religious sects prevented the fulfillment of a sense of national fraternity. It denounced religious orders as unpatriotic, violators of the law and of individual liberty, and sponsors of provincialism. It asserted that the state should be the supreme dispenser of instruction in civics and morality to its future citizens, that it should have the right to inspect and even suppress rival institutions, and that it alone should have the power to confer advanced degrees. The state should direct theological education, since it was the guardian of Science. The Church should watch over dogma, but in case of conflict, the temporal power should be supreme. The state was neutral in doctrine, but it might teach an "independent morality" in the public schools, based upon that which underlay all forms of thought. This morality might be divorced from both philosophy and religion or it might be deistic in principle. The state was also to assume charitable responsibilities.

Various agencies propagated these Jacobin ideals: assemblies of teachers, the army, the press, the Educational League, and the Freemasons. The clubs of the League carried on an active propaganda in behalf of free, compulsory, and lay primary education, freedom of association, and civic and military education. Many prominent deputies and senators were members of the League and promoted its objectives in the chambers. The organization was anti-clerical in sympathy, although its founder, Jean Macé, was a deist and denied that it was irreligious. The Freemasonry of the period, which was republican, positivistic, and anti-clerical, stirred up sentiment for the laic laws through pamphlets, lectures, and meetings. Many members of the chambers and government were Masons. Although the society theoretically did not engage in politics, individual members or lodges probably used every opportunity to further its ends.

Once in power, the republicans became increasingly intolerant of internal dissent. Their experiences during the war and Commune, their conceptions of state sovereignty, and the peril of their own position led them to adopt ruthless tactics. They discriminated against private institutions, failed to provide for freedom of instruction and freedom of association, and sometimes violated the conscience of Catholics. The danger that the "neutral" school would become a center for the propagation of the doctrines of those in power was great. Not only the Right, but men of the Left and Left Center, philosophers, writers, and clergymen protested against these policies.

The concurrence of all these forces and motives resulted in the introduction and enactment of a series of anti-clerical measures from 1876 to 1889 which foreshadowed the eventual separation of church and state and postponed consideration of constructive social legislation. . . .

The intolerant nature of much of the anti-clerical legislation of this period should not obscure the outstanding contributions which the republicans made in the direction of personal freedom and enlightenment. The enactment of a divorce law did not injure the conscience of Catholics and freed the non-Catholic from a bond in which he might not believe.

Separation of church and state by gradual processes and respect for the position of the free-thinker were in accordance with the principle of freedom of conscience. The establishment of secondary schools for girls and of free, compulsory, and lay primary education diffused culture more widely and strengthened democracy. The requirement of uniformly high qualifications for teachers and the revision of the curriculum to include scientific subjects and civics improved the quality and content of instruction.

A study of the laic legislation of the 1880's has a wider significance than is at first apparent. It is more than a tedious analysis of conditions and laws in a brief decade long since forgotten by all but the professional historian. It is an illustration of the fact that subservience to the ideal of a highly centralized national state may produce intolerance, violation of civil liberties, and suppression of the rights of autonomous groups within the state. These evils, it should be noted, may exist in a democratic republic, governed by men who once extolled individual liberties. Private educational institutions and associations differing in doctrine from those of the controlling régime are especially vulnerable to attack. The danger to religion of any political affiliation is likewise demonstrated by the history of the Church in this period. . . .

Separation — No Loss to the Church

D. W. BROGAN

THE fundamental question was that of the property rights of the Establishment. On the extreme anti-clerical side there was a desire to make the Church as poor as possible. If the clergy continued to live in the same houses and control the same buildings, what good was the separation? But Briand and the majority of the Chamber, from motives of prudence as well as of justice, were anxious to avoid

Pp. 376–8 *France Under the Republic: The Development of Modern France* (1870–1939) (New York, 1940) by D. W. Brogan. Reprinted with the permission of Harper and Row, Publishers, Incorporated and Hamish Hamilton, Ltd.

any appearance of persecution. They wished to leave the clergy in effectual control of the churches and other ecclesiastical property. But what was meant by the clergy? Was every parish to be treated as a unit? What was to happen if two persons claimed to be the priest of a parish? If the bishop was to decide, he was in effective control of the clergy and the assets — and the Pope, henceforward, would name all bishops without any voice being left to the State. To avoid this, 'religious associations' were to be set up which would be given the effective property rights in the churches, presbyteries and the rest. Priests would receive salaries for four years to come, but on a descending scale, and existing pension rights were secured. From the point of view of many Catholics, it was less rigorous than they had feared.

On the other side, Pius X condemned the Law of Separation on the ground that the law 'attributes the public celebration of religion not to the hierarchical organization divinely set up by Our Saviour, but to a lay organization.' The defenders of the law pointed out that control of the property and finances of the parishes was in lay hands in Germany. The papal objection, however, was not groundless. The German Governments recognized and enforced the authority of the bishops; they were, in any case, not hostile to the Church as such, which the French State was. Moreover a difficulty arose from the fact that, in a great many French villages and in most French towns, the real Catholics were a minority. It was possible to foresee cases where the control of the Church would be in the hands of very lukewarm Catholics indeed, a danger that did not often arise in the Rhineland or Bavaria. Yet the papal condemnation, though loyally observed, was not gladly accepted by all French laymen or even by all French bishops. The stern, unbending attitude of the Roman authorities imposed burdens not on them but on the French clergy, and the new Minister of Cults, Briand, was able to taunt the defenders of the Pope's policy in the Chamber with the notorious disagreement of the French bishops on the question of the religious associations.

What was to be done? There was no danger that the celebration of Mass would suddenly cease. Church services were treated as public meetings, but that meant asking for authorization, which the Pope forbade the clergy to do, and the simple remedy was found of abolishing the last restrictions on the right of public meeting for everybody. The use of the churches was permitted to the clergy, but they had no strict legal rights and, worse still, while the Communes could receive gifts for the upkeep of the churches of which they were now the owners, they did not need to accept them and, if they chose, could let the churches fall into ruins. The action of Pius X thus deprived the Church in France of a great deal of property and imposed great burdens on the laity.

The Church suffered far less from the separation than had been anticipated. In many districts it was difficult to recruit the clergy, but that was already an old story; some parishes had to be abandoned altogether, but this was merely the public recognition of a state of affairs barely hidden by the legal establishment. On the other hand, the effects of freedom were often bracing; a new missionary spirit was awakened among the clergy and the old bureaucratic attitude grew less common. In varied ways, the Church tackled the problem of keeping a hold on the people. It organized women's clubs in the country; it organized boy scouts; the Christian trade unions gradually freed themselves of the crippling association with the employers; and, in every department of life, the one great organization that could compete with the French State showed its renewed life. There were no schisms and few scandals. The Catholic Church was now the Church of a minority of faithful and zealous people, not the nominal and official religious organization of nearly all Frenchmen. It did not lose by the change.

A Struggle of Belief *vs* Disbelief

GEORG FRANZ

AFTER the end of the *Kulturkampf* in Prussia the great conflict between state and Catholic church, which had disturbed the whole century, returned again to its point of origin, to France. Simultaneously with the Pope's giving in to Prussia in the spring of 1880, the dark stormy petrel that had been driven from the German fields appeared over France.

The anti-church trend grew with the strengthening of the republic in France. The *Kulturkampf* in France in contrast to that in Germany was of a character inimical to the church, even seen from the point of view of the state. This was the tradition of the French Revolution which the republic continued to nurture, and the more the republican and socialist parties increased in numbers and strength, and thereby in influence on the state, the more hostile became the position of the state toward the church. Laicization was no longer an intellectual movement, but it was deeply anchored in broad segments of the population by a generation-long revolutionary tradition. Not only the workers under socialist influence were anti-church; the peasants also displayed a wide-spread religious indifference. . . .

In spite of these measures [laic laws 1880–1886] the Pope concerned himself with a friendly relationship with France. These efforts were part of his great governing program of reconciling the church with modern civilization; "Christianization of the republic and of democracy was his goal." When all his attempts at conciliation with Italy failed, Pope Leo XIII tried all the harder in the 1890's to reach a friendly understanding with France. The Pope approved the proposal of the Archbishop of Algiers that the French clergy should accept the republic. In a letter of Cardinal-Secretary Rampolla of January 5, 1892, to the Archbishop of Paris the summons was made to place the safeguarding of the interests of the church on the foundation of the republican constitution. The French Episcopate thereupon gave up its opposition to the republican state.

The great swing of Papal world policy from the Triple Alliance of the Central Powers to the Dual Alliance of France and Russia coincided exactly with the conclusion of the French-Russian treaty (1892); in the year 1895 a Russian legation was established at the Vatican. But the hopes of the great Diplomat Pope in respect to France were not fulfilled. He himself lived only to see the beginning of the final rupture, which was begun by the Associations law of 1901. The rapprochement between France and Italy gave a mighty impetus to church-hostile liberalism and Freemasonry, and made an end to the reconciliation policy of the Pope in France. Waldeck-Rousseau, a moderate Republican, had as Premier (1899-1902) begun the *Kulturkampf* by the above mentioned law. His radical successor, Emile Combes, as head of a Left government from 1902–1905 carried through in the sharpest fashion the *Kulturkampf* against the Catholic church. Until this time the French governments, in spite of general hostility to the church on political grounds, had still always valued good relations with the Vatican and had fought shy of cancelling the Concordat. Unfriendly measures, such as the closure of monastic schools, had been ac-

From Georg Franz, *Kulturkampf. Staat und Katholische Kirche in Mitteleuropa von der Säkularisation bis zum Abschluss des Preussischen Kulturkampfes.* (Munich: Verlag Georg D. W. Callwey, 1954), pp. 280–283. (Trans. Ernst and Louise Helmreich.) Reprinted by permission of the publisher.

cepted by the Curia with the greatest reluctance in the hope that a final break might be avoided. The papal election after the death of Leo XIII in 1903, also gave the leader of the Curia, Cardinal Secretary Rampolla, who was considered the most likely candidate for the chair of St. Peter, cause to avoid any sharpening of relations with France in order to assure for himself French influence at the conclave.

With the Combes Cabinet that way of thinking had come to power, because, to the cabinet, *Kulturkampf* was not a dispute with the church as a rival governing power, but was a struggle between belief and disbelief. Combes himself was a radical atheist and saw his duty in waging open war "against the Church and Faith." Accordingly there followed under his leadership in 1905 the final separation of state and church in France, the complete elimination of clerical instruction [in the

schools] and the dissolution of clerical orders. Diplomatic relations with the Vatican were broken in 1904. After the fall of the Combes' ministry the execution of the Separation Law was completed by the Clemenceau Cabinet (1906–1909) and its Minister of Education, A. Briand.

Under the sign of disbelief France, "the eldest daughter of the church" had entered the nineteenth century. Waldeck-Rousseau, Emile Combes, Georges Clemenceau, Aristide Briand carried on what the revolutionaries Danton, Marras, Robespierre had begun: under the sign of ungodliness the state had entered into the new century.

Emile Combes explained to Prince Bülow that Bismarck had started the *Kulturkampf* incorrectly, in that he had attacked the Roman Curia, which was unconquerable; "we, however, have started the war against God and we will win."

The Dechristianization of France

ADRIEN DANSETTE

THE whole of this book is in effect devoted to answering the question whether France was dechristianized under the Third Republic. The changing relationship between Church and State, the regulations governing education, the attitudes of the various political parties, the movements of opinion, and Catholic social action together provide part of the answer. But to find out whether Frenchmen as a whole have changed in their attitude to the religious problem, we must examine their attitude to life. The Frenchman is not an isolated unit. His life is influenced by the policies of successive governments, by the techniques of modern civilization, and by the habits of his own social class

— whether the peasantry, the working class or the middle class. It is also affected by the structure of the community, such as the family or the parish, of which he forms part. Each of these factors affects to some degree the outlook and feelings of the individual concerned.

While political power was in the hands of the secular republicans, politics played an essential part in the process of dechristianization that was, as we have seen, at work from the 1789 Revolution onwards. The speed of the process varied at different times, being extremely rapid at some periods and hardly perceptible at others. When they were in control of the parliamentary machine, these republicans con-

From Dansette, *op. cit.*; vol. II, pp. 414–417; 421–22. Reprinted by permission of the publisher.

structed a system of laws secularizing the official, social, and private lives of French citizens. Without re-examining these laws in detail, we should perhaps indicate the contribution to the dechristianization of the country made by the more important of them, which related to education. The law of 1880 forbade religious teaching in State schools, while that of 1886 removed from these schools the teachers belonging to religious orders. The teachers' training colleges were re-organized and increased in numbers and formed a new body of teachers imbued with an entirely different spirit. Catholic teachers disappeared gradually from the field of public education and by 1914 the great majority of their successors owed no allegiance whatever to the Church. While most of the members of this majority were scrupulous in observing religious neutrality, many, whose numbers cannot be accurately assessed, made no secret of their fundamental hostility to Catholicism. It was a hostility, moreover, that was sustained by the religious quarrels and provoked or increased by the antipathy with which teachers in State schools were regarded in the areas in which Catholicism was strong. These, however, were exceptional cases. In general terms the effect of the educational reforms in the various communes was to place alongside the representative of religion one who represented indifference or irreligion.

What was the influence of such men? It might be thought that their pupils were too young to understand the bearing of the teaching on religious matters. But the first religious notions of the children were derived not so much from a direct appeal to their minds and an attempt to influence their judgement as from the slow penetration of ideas, hardly at the conscious level at all. These they imbibed mainly within the family circle, but the teacher, with an outlook alien to religion and a vocabulary in which religious terms such as God, soul, and prayer had no place, also played his part in determining the approach of the children. The actual extent of his influence

is difficult to determine. It may have been greatest at the point where it became indirect, when the memories of the earlier years in the classroom took on their full significance for the adolescent mind, enabling it to appreciate the incompatibility between the teaching received in school and the Church's teaching. The teacher, who knew as much as the parish priest, got along without religion, and perhaps he was right.

The teacher's role was not restricted to the school. Often, being the only person in the district capable of interpreting the circulars sent out by the prefect, he acted as clerk to the local authority. He was frequently the most important man in the village and in any case one whose opinion counted and whose advice was sought in any trouble.

The second series of secular laws, passed in the years between 1901 and 1908, had an equally marked dechristianizing effect. Members of religious orders, forced to disperse or go into exile, were no longer able to carry on any pastoral work or to teach. But the most immediately disastrous measure was the separation law. Whatever we may think of this law and however fortunate its effects may appear in retrospect, it has to be admitted that the immediate result was to increase the speed of the dechristianization. The State declared that from that time forth it no longer took any cognizance of the institution that was from the Catholic's point of view the most important of all because it guided him towards his eternal destiny. This indifference itself amounted to a denial. The philosophical significance of the law was no doubt beyond the understanding of the great mass of French people. But country people who had an innate respect for officialdom, for the established order, and for legal enactments, no longer felt themselves obliged to respect a Church on which the State had finally turned its back, after having first treated it with severity. In the eyes of the ordinary man, the churchmen must have been guilty of something rather bad in order to merit being treated in such a way, and he wondered as a corollary why he should himself be expected to treat the Church any better than the authorities had done. Personal interest was an added factor for all those whose position depended on the State. Cases were noted of school teachers who ceased to go to Mass once the laws in question were passed, but who had previously gone to church and made some parade of following in their prayer books. They had come to the conclusion that this was no longer worth doing or else that such an attitude might do them harm. In areas of occasional conformity — that is those places where it was usual to go to church only for baptisms, first communions, marriages, and funerals — there was a definite decline in the level of religious practice. In some places it was catastrophic. In Limoges the proportion of children not baptized rose from 2.5 per cent in 1899 to 33.9 per cent in 1914. Civil marriages were 14 per cent of the total in 1899 and 59.8 per cent in 1915. The greater harmony in the religious field after the first world war was, however, followed by some return to religious practice in those areas of occasional conformity in which the deterioration had been most marked. As was to be expected, the separation had little effect on true Catholics and in the areas in which Catholicism had remained staunch, the faith was maintained without weakness.

The effects of the law were accentuated by the action of the administrative authorities responsible for applying it. They reserved the appointments at their disposal for those of whose outlook they approved and were not slow to annoy and persecute those of whom they disapproved.

Politics in general and the system of secular education in particular are normally almost exclusively blamed for the dechristianization of France because their influence was felt directly. Less attention is paid to other factors, doubtless even more important but affecting religious life only indirectly. We are thinking of modern techniques together with their economic and social consequences. . . .

The railways, the bicycle, the motor car, the motor coach, and the newspaper, in fact mechanical civilization in all its aspects, acted as an instrument of dechristianization by increasing human contacts and encouraging the circulation of goods and ideas. But it can no more be regarded as pagan in itself than the horse and the ship, which favoured the spread of Christianity by performing a similar role in the last years of the Roman Empire, can be regarded as Christian. These modern techniques did, however, upset long established patterns of life and created a hitherto unknown economic and social environment. The Church was accustomed to these old ways of life because it belonged to the social structure of which they were the expression. To avoid suffering from the extension of modern techniques the Church would therefore have had to make a simultaneous effort to adapt itself, to assimilate these techniques and use them for its own ends, just as it had used the old techniques they were replacing. It would have had to adapt its own structure to conform with the new economic and social structure of society and rejuvenate a message which, immutable though it is, had become out-of-date in its mode of expression and accent. At the beginning, the Church in France was too conservative in outlook to make or even to envisage the necessary effort, which would in any case have been difficult for so ancient and massive an institution.

The Decline of Anti-Clericalism

ALBERT GUÉRARD

Iᴛs [the Separation Law] effects on the religious life of the country were excellent. The Concordat had made the Church somnolent; with freedom from official trammels there came a magnificent revival of thought and fervor. Catholic philosophers such as Leroy, Sertillanges, Jacques Maritain renewed a tradition long in abeyance. Catholic novelists such as François Mauriac, Catholic poets such as Paul Claudel were in the forefront of literature. There were a number of significant conversions. At no time since the Middle Ages was church building so active as between the two world wars. As soon as the threat of clericalism disappeared, anti-clericalism sickened. After the death of the uncompromising pope, Pius X, a *modus vivendi* was reached. The Church did accept the Separation Law: the only concession by the State was that the Associations for Public Worship were formed on a diocesan basis instead of using the township or commune as a unit. Diplomatic relations were resumed between Paris and the Vatican. Napoleon himself had come to consider the Concordat as his worst mistake: after over a hundred years the error was corrected at last.

From Albert Guérard, *France: A Modern History* (Ann Arbor: University of Michigan Press, 1959), p. 365. Reprinted by permission of the publisher.

CONCLUSION

In this collection of readings, attention is focused on the reaction within the church to modern society, and secondly on the readjustment of relations between the church and the modern state in Italy, Germany, and France. In other states similar controversies also occurred; in some states they were postponed until after the World Wars. The conflicts grew out of the past; the settlements reached helped shape the ever-changing nature of modern civilization.

More questions than answers arise from a survey of church-state relations such as this, and therein lies much of its value. While some of the issues of that time are no longer acute, most of the basic problems remain. Is religious toleration a sound ideal, and what is necessary to its implementation? What is required for the achievement of the goal set by Cavour, "A Free Church in a Free State"? Is it to the advantage of either church or state to have political parties based on any particular religious ideology? Is it possible, to borrow a phrase from a United States Supreme Court ruling, to erect a wall between the affairs of the church and those of the state? What obligations does a church have to the state and the state to the church? Should the churches govern themselves or should the state share in the active administration of the church as was, and still is, the regular practice in many European states? Is the concept of a religiously neutral state the proper one? And, one might ask, is the religiously neutral state basically anti-religious, bearing in mind the biblical quotation that he who is not with me is against me? Is the religiously neutral state the first step towards the religiously hostile state which appeared in Europe for the first time since the French Revolution after World War I? Where is the line between state support and neutrality, or between neutrality and hostility?

If the state is not to be just a police state, but also a cultural force, how far should it go in promoting social services, the arts, and religion in general? Should a state continue to grant tax exemption to the churches, a practice that goes far back in history? If it does, should such exemption be extended to all property held by churches such as parson-ages, school buildings, apartment houses, and industrial enterprises? Does the state have the right or duty to inquire into church finances; for example, how the churches raise and spend money for charitable purposes? Should the state undertake special protection for the observance of Sunday and other religious holidays? If it does so for Sunday, should it make similar regulations for the Sabbath?

In the field of education, the right of the state to impose compulsory education was for many years strenuously opposed by some churchmen, who held that the church and the family alone were to determine the education of the young. If the state permits private and parochial schools, should these be granted public tax funds? Does the state have the right to set standards for such schools and require that certain subjects be taught and the instruction be carried out in a particular language? Should the state abolish religious instruction, Bible readings, and prayer in the public schools, especially if such practices are supported by parents and local customs? What if religious tenets forbid observance of certain state regulations such as a pledge of allegiance, or compulsory immunization against infectious diseases? Just what is covered by religious rights and the "freedom of religion"? Aside from education, in regard to other family matters, are the establishment of civil marriage and divorce, the dissemination of birth control information, the legalization of abortion, the regulation of burials and cemeteries an illegitimate intervention of the state in the religious field?

There are also equally vexatious problems regarding the role of the churches in relation to the state. Should they be expected to offer prayers regularly on behalf of the state and the persons in authority, a long-standing custom and a practice recognized in the concordats concluded by the Vatican? Do the churches have the right, or perhaps even the duty, to insist that the state respect an individual's conscientious objection to serve in the armed forces? Should they cooperate in the maintenance of the corps of chaplains in the armed services and, on the other hand, does the state have any obligations in regard to providing such religious services? Should churches protest against the use of atomic bombs, saturation bombing of civilian populations, or other specific acts of war? Should they raise their voices for the righting of social evils and the protection of minorities? Is it a function of the churches to press the state to legislate in regard to censorship of films, the theater, literature, or in general act as the guardian of morality? Should the churches issue public pronouncements on public issues of the day, or restrict themselves to the "cure of souls" as Hitler maintained? Just how active should the churches be in trying to influence state action? In relation to this problem it might be well to weigh the words of Konstantin Petrovich Pobedonostsev, the famous Procurator of the Holy Synod of Russia and an ardent opponent of the separation of church and state: "No church which retains the consciousness of its own worthiness will ever surrender its lawful influence on the family or on civil society. To demand that the church shall abstain from intervention in civil affairs is scarcely to give it new strength" (*Reflections of a Russian Statesman*, pp. 10—11).

These are but a few of the questions and problems which arise out of the relationship between church and state in modern society. That they exist cannot be denied; that they are controversial is patent. What their ultimate solution and adjustment involves is a vital matter for study and debate. The experience of Italy, Germany, and France in the period from 1864 to 1914 may help to throw light on the continuing problem of church-state relations today.

SUGGESTIONS FOR ADDITIONAL READING

Additional pages in the books from which selections have been taken, none of which are listed in this bibliographical note, will provide excellent further reading. Other books of a general nature are those by the biographer of Pius IX, E. E. Y. Hales, *Revolution and Papacy 1769—1846* (New York, 1960) and *The Catholic Church in the Modern World. A Survey from the French Revolution to the Present* (New York, 1958); Raymond Corrigan, *The Church and the Nineteenth Century* (Milwaukee, 1938); Carl C. Eckhardt, *The Papacy and World Affairs as Reflected in the Secularization of Politics* (Chicago, 1937); Jerome G. Kerwin, *Catholic Viewpoint on Church and State* (New York, 1960); James MacCaffrey, *History of the Church in the Nineteenth Century* (2 vols., Dublin, 1909); Joseph N. Moody, ed., *Church and Society: Catholic Social and Political Thought and Movements, 1789—1950* (New York, 1953); Thomas G. Sanders, *Protestant Concepts of Church and State: Historical Backgrounds and Approaches for the Future* (Garden City, N.Y., 1963); Luigi Sturzo, *Church and State* (New York, 1939). There is a good summary of religious problems in Ch. IV of Carlton J. H. Hayes, *A Generation of Materialism 1871—1900* (New York, 1941). Robert A. Graham, *Vatican Diplomacy. A Study of Church and State on the International Plane* (Princeton, 1959), is a ground-breaking study of the Pope as a sovereign ruler. Two of the best books on canon law are: John A. Abbo and Jerome D. Hannan, *The Sacred Canons. A Concise Presentation of the Current Disciplinary Norms of the Church*, (rev. ed., St. Louis, 1960) and T. Lincoln Bouscaren and Adam C. Ellis, *Canon Law. A Text and Commentary* (3rd ed., Milwaukee, 1958). Francis J. Powers, ed., *Papal Pronouncements on the Political Order* (Westminster, Maryland, 1952), covers the period from Leo XIII in 1878 to Pius XII in 1951.

The Syllabus, the Vatican Council, and Papal Infallibility are touched upon in most of the volumes cited in this survey. Two famous essays by a prominent French bishop should be noted: Mgr. Dupanloup, *La Convention du 15 Septembre et l'Encyclique du 8 Décembre* (Paris, 1865) and his *Observations sur la controverse soulevée relativement à la définition de l'infaillibilité au futur concile* (Paris, 1869). The Council itself is treated fully in: Cuthbert Butler, *The Vatican Council* (2 vols., London, 1930); E. Ollivier, *L'Église et l'État au Concile de Vatican* (2 vols., Paris, 1879); Johann Friedrich, *Geschichte des vatikanischen Konzils* (3 vols., Bonn, 1877—1887); T. Granderath, *Geschichte des vatikanischen Konzils* (5 vols., Freiburg, 1903—1906); see also George Gordon Coulton, *Papal Infallibility* (London, 1932). The part played by the American hierarchy at the Vatican Council is covered in very readable fashion in James J. Hennesey, *The First Council of the Vatican: The American Experience* (New York, 1963). Lord Acton's essay on "The Vatican Council" first published in the *North British Review* (1870) is reprinted in *The History of Freedom and Other Essays*, ed. by J. N. Figgis and R. V. Laurence (London, 1909). Other pertinent essays by Acton, among them those on "Ultramontanism," "The States of the Church," and "The Munich Congress [Old Catholics]" are collected in *Essays on Church and State*, ed. by Douglas Woodruff (New York, 1953). Other polemical essays which aroused much attention in England and the United States are: W. E. Gladstone, *Vaticanism: An Answer to Reproofs and Replies* (New York, 1875); W. E. Gladstone, *Speeches of Pope Pius IX* (New York, 1875), a review and analysis, originally published in the *Quarterly Review* January 1875, of two volumes of discourses by Pius IX. See also W. E. Gladstone, *Correspondence on Church and State*, ed. by D. C. Lathbury (2 vols., New York, 1911); Henry Edward Manning, Archbishop of Westminster, *The Vatican Council and its Definitions: A Pastoral Letter* (New York, 1871); H. E. Manning, *The Vatican Decrees in their Bearing on Civil Allegiance* [A reply to "The Vatican Decrees, etc.," by the Right Hon. W. E. Gladstone] (London, 1875); "The True Story of the Vatican Council," *The Nineteenth Century*, I (1877), 122—140, 177—197, 479—503, 597—610, 790—808; J. H. Newman, *A Letter Addressed to His Grace the Duke of Norfolk on Occasion of*

112

Mr. Gladstone's recent Expostulation (New York, 1875). Biographies of leading churchmen of the different countries in this period are most useful but all these cannot be listed here. Significant studies of the Popes of the period are: R. Aubert, *Le pontificat de Pie IX* (Paris, 1952), excellent bibliography; R. P. Lecanuet, *La vie de l'Église sous Léon XIII* (Paris, 1930); Eduardo Soderini, *Il pontificato di Leone XIII* (3 vols., Milan, 1932–1933). Two volumes of this work have been translated into English by Barbara Carter as *The Pontificate of Leo XIII* (London, 1934), and *Leo XIII, Italy and France* (London, 1935), while the third volume has been translated into German by Richard Bauersfeld as *Leo XIII und der deutsche Kulturkampf, nach dem römischen Archiven bearbeitet* (Vienna, 1935). Important volumes on Vatican relations with two of the great powers of Europe in this period may best be listed here: Friedrich Engel-Janosi, *Osterreich und der Vatikan 1846–1918* (2 vols., Vienna, 1958–60); Eduard Winter, *Russland und das Papstum*, Part 2, *Von der Aufklärung bis zur grossen sozialistischen Oktoberrevolution* (Berlin, 1961).

Other useful volumes on church and state relations in Italy are: S. William Halperin, *The Separation of Church and State in Italian Thought from Cavour to Mussolini* (Chicago, 1937); Janet P. Trevelyan, *A Short History of the Italian People* (4th ed., New York, 1956); R. Albrecht-Carrié, *Italy from Napoleon to Mussolini* (New York, 1950); William Roscoe Thayer, *The Life and Times of Cavour* (2 vols., New York, 1911); R. de Cesare, *The Last Days of Papal Rome, 1850–1870* (London, 1909); Stefano Jacini, *La crisi religiosa del Risorgimento: la politica ecclesiastica italiana da Villafranca a Porta Pia* (Bari, 1938). Useful introductory chapters on the period from 1914 are presented in D. A. Binchy, *Church and State in Fascist Italy* (Oxford, 1941) and V. E. Orlando, *Rome vs Rome*, trans. from the Italian by Clarence Beardslee (New York, 1937).

Attention is called to the excellent bibliographies in the recent histories of the *Kulturkampf* by Georg Franz and Erich Schmidt-Volkmar (See Section III). Other general histories are: Johannes Kissling, *Geschichte des Kulturkampfes im Deutschen Reich* (3 vols., Freiburg, 1911–1916); Georges Goyau, *Bismarck et l'église. Le culturkampf* (4 vols., Paris, 1911–13); Rudolph Lill, *Die Wende im Kulturkampf: Leo XIII, Bismarck und die Zentrumspartei 1878–1880* (Tübingen, 1973). Adelheid Constabel, ed., *Die Vorgeschichte des Kulturkampfes. Quellenveröffentlichung aus dem Deutschen Zentralarchiv* (2 ed., Berlin, 1957) published by the German Democratic Republic, has an excellent introduction by Fritz Hartung. The opening chapters of Ernst C. Helmreich's *The German Churches Under Hitler: Background, Struggle, and Epilogue* (Detroit, 1978) give a brief survey of church-state problems in Germany from the Reformation down to the end of the Empire. All general histories of the German Empire as well as biographies of Bismarck necessarily touch on the *Kulturkampf.* Among the many biographies of German leaders of the period the following are selected: Erich Eyck, *Bismarck. Leben und Werk* (3 vols., Zürich, 1941–1944); Adalbert Wahl, *Vom Bismarck der 70er Jahre* (Tübingen, 1920); Raymond Beazley, "Bismarck and the Papacy under Leo XIII," *Quarterly Review*, 288 (1950), 536–547; Johann Friedrich, *Ignaz von Döllinger* (3 vols., Munich, 1898–1901); Walter Reichle, *Zwischen Staat und Kirche. Das Leben und Wirken des preussischen Kultusministers Heinrich von Mühler* (Berlin, 1938); Erich Förster, *Adalbert Falk. Sein Leben und Wirken als Preussicher Kultusminister* (Gotha, 1927). Books dealing with some special aspects of the *Kulturkampf* period are: J. F. v. Schulte, *Der Altkatholizismus* (Giessen, 1887); C. B. Moss, *The Old Catholic Movement, its Origin and History* (London, 1948); Heinrich Bornkamm, *Die Staatsidee im Kulturkampf* (Munich, 1950); George G. Windell, *The Catholics and German Unity 1866–1871* (Minneapolis, 1954); Ernst C. Helmreich, *Religious Education in German Schools: An Historical Approach* (Cambridge, 1959); M. Orestes Kolbeck, *American Opinion on the Kulturkampf 1871–1882* (Washington, 1942).

For many years the standard account of church-state relations in France was A. Debidour, *L'Église catholique et l'État sous la troisième République 1870–1906* (2 vols., Paris, 1906–1909). Other pertinent volumes are: C. de Montalembert, *L'Église libre dans l'État libre* (Paris, 1863); Anatole France, *L'Église de la République* (Paris, 1904); Edouard Lecanuet, *Les signes avant-coureurs de la séparation; les dernières annés de Leo XIII et l'avènement de Pie X, 1894–1910*

(Paris, 1930); Clarence E. Elwell, *The Influence of the Enlightenment on the Catholic Theory of Religious Education in France 1750—1850* (Cambridge, 1944); J. E. C. Bodley, *The Church in France* (London, 1906); Alfred Rambaud, *Jules Ferry* (Paris, 1903); John McManners, *Church and State in France 1870—1914* (New York, 1972); Maurice Larkin, *Church and State after the Dreyfus Affair: The Separation Issue in France* (New York, 1974). Of a more monographic nature is Malcolm O. Partin's *Waldeck-Rousseau, Combes and the Church: The Politics of Anticlericalism, 1899—1905* (Durham, N.C., 1969). General histories of the Third Republic, which must touch on church-state relations to some extent, are not cited here. Nor is an attempt made to suggest books on the much-discussed Boulanger and Dreyfus crises, which are close to the topic at hand. The first thirty-six pages of Harry W. Paul, *The Second Ralliement: The Rapprochement between Church and State in France in the Twentieth Century* (Washington, D.C., 1967) give an excellent summary of church and state in France from the Revolution to the close of World War I. The heart of the volume is devoted to the denouement of church-state conflict in the 1920's. Some studies on other related topics are: Roger H. Soltau, *French Political Thought in the Nineteenth Century* (New Haven, 1931); R. H. Soltau, *French Parties and Politics 1871—1921* (London, 1930); Mildred J. Headings, *French Freemasonry under the Third Republic* (Baltimore, 1949); Robert F. Byrnes, *Antisemitism in Modern France*, vol. I, *The Prologue to the Dreyfus Affair* (New Brunswick, 1950); Samuel M. Osgood, *French Royalism under the Third and Fourth Republics* (The Hague, 1960).